TRANSFORMING BEHAVIOUR
in the
CLASSROOM

SAGE was founded in 1965 by Sara Miller McCune to support the dissemination of usable knowledge by publishing innovative and high-quality research and teaching content. Today, we publish over 900 journals, including those of more than 400 learned societies, more than 800 new books per year, and a growing range of library products including archives, data, case studies, reports, and video. SAGE remains majority-owned by our founder, and after Sara's lifetime will become owned by a charitable trust that secures our continued independence.

Los Angeles | London | New Delhi | Singapore | Washington DC

Geoffrey James

TRANSFORMING
BEHAVIOUR
in the
CLASSROOM

*a solution-focused
guide for
new teachers*

Los Angeles | London | New Delhi
Singapore | Washington DC

Los Angeles | London | New Delhi
Singapore | Washington DC

SAGE Publications Ltd
1 Oliver's Yard
55 City Road
London EC1Y 1SP

SAGE Publications Inc.
2455 Teller Road
Thousand Oaks, California 91320

SAGE Publications India Pvt Ltd
B 1/I 1 Mohan Cooperative Industrial Area
Mathura Road
New Delhi 110 044

SAGE Publications Asia-Pacific Pte Ltd
3 Church Street
#10-04 Samsung Hub
Singapore 049483

Editor: James Clark
Editorial assistant: Robert Patterson
Production editor: Nicola Marshall
Copyeditor: Solveig Gardner Servian
Proofreader: Sarah Cooke
Indexer: Silvia Benvenuto
Marketing manager: Dilhara Attygalle
Cover design: Naomi Robinson
Typeset by: C&M Digitals (P) Ltd, Chennai, India
Printed and bound by CPI Group (UK) Ltd,
Croydon, CR0 4YY

Library of Congress Control Number: 2015942960

British Library Cataloguing in Publication data

A catalogue record for this book is available from
the British Library

ISBN 978-1-47390-230-5
ISBN 978-1-47390-231-2 (pbk)

CONTENTS

ABOUT THE AUTHOR

I started teaching in my mid-forties, on supply in mainstream schools and then on the staff of a special school, full of hope and ideas. Before that I'd been a research biologist, a small-scale farmer and an outdoor educator for people with learning disabilities, among other things. After a few years' class teaching, I moved to the educational support service for a local authority, where I worked on my PhD exploring the field of behaviour. When I stepped into teaching twenty years ago I could see the need to do something different from the old failing routines of punishment and control.

Finding a way to teach better behaviour in a creative and exciting way rather than trying to stamp out bad behaviour by force has made a remarkable difference to me as a working teacher and to the many people – adults and children – who I've worked with. If behaviour is seen as a force to be resisted, it can be exhausting trying to withstand and defeat it. In the course of ten years of research and practice I met up with a way of looking for what's working rather than what's failing, for what makes people happy and successful in the face of difficulty. It is called 'solution-focused thinking' and it's led to some of the best work I have done in my life and to this book. To start with I thought students' success must be a fluke, but successes piled up and convinced me that this idea is something of usefulness and importance.

Over the years I've taken the solution-focused approach into many different situations, to find out just what it can do; individual behaviour support; training professionals in the solution-focused approach; child and adolescent mental health services; organizational and management development; social work training; coaching; team building; and behaviour support and peer coaching in schools. The solution-focused approach and practical solution-support have the potential to produce happiness and success wherever problems occur.

A head teacher said one day when I was leaving after completing work with a student, 'When we want another miracle, we'll call you'. That's what it sometimes may look like, but it's more than that; in schools it is a form of systematic and well-structured good teaching that brings results. It just happens to be about behaviour.

Geoffrey James

FOREWORD

I have been asked to write a note about this book as a teacher using solution-support successfully. Having seen the approach in action, with support but no direct training, I am putting the approach into action in my infant school.

As a teacher I feel strongly about learning, in particular, how children learn. Enabling children to develop skills which promote their curiosity and interest in learning has been important to me for a long time. However, more recently I have become more aware of the significance of other factors, such as motivation, perseverance and the sense to which a child believes they can make the difference, their perceived self-efficacy.

As a school this has caused us to reflect on many areas of our practice. The biggest challenge for us was in addressing the way we used rewards, stickers and praise; something that we'd learnt to accept and promote as 'good practice'. However, we decided that our use of these needed to be reviewed, in our drive to foster a level of independence in the way children make positive decisions about all areas of their learning. The result, several years on, is that rewards and praise are used purposefully and much less. Over time we've come to see that focusing the child's attention on the effort they're investing is helping to achieve many of the areas above that we've come to value.

However, it was on reflecting upon how we viewed different areas of learning that resulted in the biggest shift in our thinking. This wasn't an overnight revelation but came during a period when we were exploring how we fostered academic learning compared to social and emotional learning.

For some time we had made many changes in the way we promoted learning in the classroom and the gradual shift towards developing effective learning behaviours was starting to have a significant impact. However, while our classroom practice was developing strongly, a wide gap was emerging between this and the way we responded to mistakes and miscues in children's social and emotional learning – or their behaviour. In short, when children made mistakes with their academic learning, such as with their reading or writing skills, it was viewed as an opportunity to identify their next steps or targets; however, mistakes in social and emotional learning, particularly when it impacted upon other children, were still dealt with through punitive and deficit models whereby children would lose rewards or free time.

It was coming to understand and view behaviour as outcomes of a child's social and emotional development, and that all learning is inherently a cognitive process, that prompted this change. We needed to respond to all mistakes in a consistent manner, and this meant challenging many of the entrenched viewpoints about behaviour, many of which were driven by the need for justice, rather than helping a child to prevent further reoccurrences.

It was at this time we met Geoffrey, who had agreed to work with a child who was finding coping with many areas of school life challenging, mainly due to the high levels of anxiety they experienced. Over the coming weeks we saw signs that the child was relaxing and starting to cope more successfully in school. Notably their levels of anxiety decreased as they started to develop an awareness that they could influence change in their own life.

From discussions with Geoffrey, over a period of time I started to understand the way he worked with children using the solution-focused approach to the work, particularly the simplicity of the techniques and how the subtleties of the language used resulted in paradigm shifts in children's thinking. Eager to capitalize on this learning I started to use the approach, usually with children who were not responding to other strategies.

Since these early encounters, our work and thinking has continued to be strongly influenced by those early conversations with Geoffrey and experiences with children. Conversations focus on enabling children to see what they are achieving and almost always result in their inevitable realization that they have engineered the change that has enabled them to succeed, sowing the seeds that grow and flower as self-efficacy.

While for us there is still much more to learn, recently hearing one child offer a younger child the possibility that they were being 'successful' rather than 'good', the term the younger child had used, highlights how our work is able to change the way children view themselves and others. The same younger child is starting to believe that they can bring about the change they want to see, to enable them to cope better in school. I am working with this 6-year-old child at the moment, who is responding really well and has finally learnt to say 'successful' and is slowly understanding what this means. A few days ago I dropped the golden question 'What is it about you ...?' to see if the child can think about what it is about personally, and which strengths and resources led to success – this is still such a hard question to tackle!

While the journey is often 'two steps forward and one step back', having an approach which opens up conversations where we can celebrate that we're still 'one step further forward' is liberating for both myself and the children I work with.

The idea of replacing failure and punishment with success and a growing sense of self-efficacy in children has brought more happiness into our lives and a new professional dynamic into our school. This book gives you the opportunity to walk this path and I can recommend it to you.

Andy Tovell, Headteacher

PREFACE

I have written this book as a guide for new teachers working in either primary or secondary education, on an approach that has the potential to transform behaviour in schools. The book is an inquiry into behaviour, aimed at developing understanding and practice together. We will be rethinking some common assumptions and opening up a new practical approach to changing behaviour. As with any teaching, it is only your own motivation to learn and to develop as a learner that can bring the hopes expressed in this book to fruition. As a teacher, I understand your need as a learner to sense your own autonomy, expertise and purpose in the journey we are starting here. My role is to walk with you along this path, as your guide and mentor, through the course of the book and into your classroom. Let's get started.

Chapter 1 explores general aspects of behaviour management and introduces the concept of the solution-focused approach to behaviour and making connections between theory and practice in relation to teaching behaviour. Chapter 2 'What do we mean by behaviour?' asks you to rethink behaviour as an aspect of overall learning and teaching rather than as a separate category of problems to be managed. It does this by exploring the connections between your values and beliefs and your practice in teaching behaviour.

Chapter 3 'Becoming the best teacher you can be' covers planning classroom management and incorporating solution-focused teaching as a pedagogical inquiry approach to changing behaviour. Chapter 4 'Developing confidence in practice', explores what can affect your confidence in your role as a teacher of behaviour, and offers guidance on making plans to strengthen and grow your practice.

Chapter 5 'Making sense of behaviour problems' looks at how you can identify what type of behaviour problem you are dealing with and the best problem-solving approach to take. Chapter 6 'Being solution focused in school' offers an introduction to the structure of solution-support and taking the first steps in its use.

Chapter 7 'Talking about pedagogy' reflects on the important teaching concept of pedagogy and makes connections with teaching for behaviour change. Chapter 8 'Motivation and changing behaviour' considers how change is motivated and how you can support student motivation to change behaviour.

Chapter 9 'Changing habits and changing thinking' explores what might be going on in the inside when you take a particular approach to a student's changing behaviour.

Chapter 10 'The practical work of changing behaviour' builds on the earlier chapters of the book to provide a practical framework for applying a solution-focused approach to your teaching. It draws together your new learning and practice, strengthening your clear, practical understanding of solution-support and reflecting on its application in your own circumstances.

Evidence of change

Throughout this book I will be offering you evidence about the effectiveness of solution-support as a teaching approach to changing behaviour. The first piece of this practice-based evidence is in the form of a letter from a mother, addressed to me about work that her young son Adam and I did together. It was straightforward solution-support, and demonstrates the potential of this approach to produce useful change and a successful outcome in a complex situation. It was the result of study, practice and the methodical application of a teaching approach: solution-support.

Solution-focused thinking and its practical application through solution-support are at the heart of this book. The good news is that it is something you can learn to use yourself as a teacher, in real situations where you can make the kind of difference that you will read about now. You will meet Adam himself in Chapter 5.

From E. Hill to Dr Geoffrey James
February 2013

Dear Dr Geoffrey James,
Re: Adam Hill

I have left a little time to write this letter to ensure giving a true impact that your work with my son, Adam, has had. Before you met Adam, our life was very difficult and not because he was a difficult child. Almost the opposite,

(Continued)

(Continued)

Adam has always been a kind, happy, intelligent, eager-to-please, friendly little boy with no behavioural problems but safe to say probably not the most confident and quite mere-hearted. However over a period of some time (years in fact), he has become increasingly anxious around social situations and seemingly simple events which predominantly showed in his refusal to leave our home. This anxiety had major implications for him and in particular his attendance at school.

I cannot begin to explain how heartbreaking that was for me to witness; finding him curled up in a bed sobbing, hyperventilating, trying to make himself sick, hearing him cry how life would be better if he was dead or threatening to break his own legs. Late at night he would regularly be pacing the landing up and down saying over and over, 'I can't go to school tomorrow, I can't go, I'm not going, I can't go to school tomorrow, I'm not'. I was worn out and I'm quite sure he was even more so.

Can I just say that apart from being a mum, I also work in a primary school which includes special needs children, pacifying upsets, helping them to manage behaviours, and working towards their emotional progress and confidence, so I wasn't sitting back naively. I knew Adam needed something more and until you came I felt quite lonely, frustrated and really concerned in my urgency for the wellbeing of my son. His school have been very good supporting me and Adam but for months I battled with other educational professionals telling me he had attachment issues to me or he was seen as being naughty and just wanting his own way.

Then you come along. From the moment we met you, I knew you would have my full trust and Adam clearly felt this too. You explained what you would like to do, you were refreshing in your understanding and approach and I knew you would change things, and for the first time in a long time I believed, 'This is going to work'. You had an immediate rapport with Adam and quickly established you had no expectations of him, which immediately took away his anxiety of this being a 'big' thing. You also admitted to having no magic wand but you gave us both the confidence that together we were going to find a way to make this better.

Adam and I didn't really discuss what you had talked about in your time together, partly because he couldn't remember the details (which I guess shows the wonder of what you do) but he always looked forward to your meetings, which certainly made the morning's routines of those days much easier.

Moreover because you gave me complete trust to believe that you would be helping my boy, I didn't need to know everything about those meetings. In the first week of your time together there was only a minor change, but over the weeks every day got better for us. He was more rational in his thoughts and generally just calmer. You gave him the life skills so he understood that the anxiety – and however it showed itself – wasn't going to go away but HE was in control.

I clearly remember one evening and the familiar scared voice said 'It's PE tomorrow'. Calmly I reasoned 'That's not a problem is it?' He then walked to his class timetable I had put on the wall in the hallway and I quietly watched as he pointed to each lesson of the next day (which did include PE), then he turned to me and simply said 'No'. I could have cried. It may sound silly to someone who hasn't watched their child agonise, threaten their own wellbeing, cry, made themselves sick, rolled up in a ball and crouched in a corner just trying to get out of the situation they simply can't handle but it was such an emotional relief for me, perhaps more than it was for Adam at that point. From that moment, Adam has never again questioned PE or wondered how he can get out of doing it, and most situations are the same, they just happen naturally.

As January approached it was a time of breaths being held because of the long Christmas holiday but Adam went back straight after, we even had to wait for the doors to open on the first day. It's not that Adam is loving school in that sense, he's not running excitedly to the door, but he is walking in unaided and he is smiling after every day and there is no visible or verbal anxiety. He comes to the shop with me, not because he loves shopping but simply because it's not an issue. And we are all sleeping!

His personality is the same but his demeanour has changed, he is relaxed, he is a healthy ten year old and he walks and talks with an air of 'I'm happy to be me' and it's been a while since I've seen that.

He has regained a belief in his heart and a spirit to try, and that is because of you.

I thank you whole heartedly for your kindness and acumen Geoffrey, you are a special man our family will never forget. I wish you many more years helping families as you have ours.

Yours sincerely,
Eileen Hill and Adam

How did that happen? You will find out as you read on.

ACKNOWLEDGEMENTS

I am very grateful for the encouragement and support that has been so kindly given to me over many years by all of my close family, to Professor Ivor Goodson who opened a door, smiling, to Evan George and Harvey Ratner, and other solution-focused partners in many places. I've been propped up and constructively criticized by my friends Drs Jeremy and Janet Anscombe, Tim Greenhill, Colin Stanwell-Smith, Tim Taylor, and my writing has been fully enabled by James Clark and the team at SAGE.

And as a final note, I'm ever grateful to Steve de Shazer and Insoo Kim Berg who had the vision to think and to do something different, to go looking for solutions and who left us with questions.

You can contact me through my website www.solution-support.co.uk and I welcome every opportunity to talk about solution-focused work, at any level of detail.

1

INTRODUCTION

Transforming behaviour in the classroom: a solution-focused guide for new teachers

This chapter will give you the opportunity to:

- explore some general aspects of behaviour management
- introduce the concept of solution-focused approaches to behaviour
- emphasize the importance of making connections between theory and practice

I would like to introduce you to Owen. He is 15, with a short crewcut, bright blue eyes, a lean and compact build and a reputation for fighting. School incident reports say he is aggressive and has anger problems. He has been in trouble with the police, and he has been all the way through the school's behaviour policy. Recently he has been told that he will be permanently excluded if he doesn't stop fighting and start behaving, but it does not seem to have any effect.

In turn I had been told about the problems, and about the school's suggestion that he needs an anger management course. I had been shown the pile of incident slips recording his failings, but when I met him I put all this to one side, because I am interested in finding out about something else.

I wanted to hear about his plans for his future, about his best hopes for school.

Me: 'Owen, what's your best hope for school? You've got the rest of this year to go and I'm wondering about what's your best hope?'

Owen: 'Well ... not get kicked out.'

Does that surprise you? He'd been told often enough that if he didn't behave himself, he would be excluded, but he hadn't made any effort to change.

Me: 'So what might happen instead?'

Owen: Stay in school.'

Me: 'So what might change a bit, for you to be sure that you stay in school?'

Owen: 'Stop fighting I suppose.'

Me: 'Suppose you did that, how would that be good for you?'

Owen: 'Well, I want to join the Army when I leave school, and I need a good report. I've been in trouble with fighting and if I get into trouble with the police again, the Army won't take me.'

So that's Owen's goal, and his plan for how to get there. It's given us the focus for our work together. Now I'd like to know more about his successes.

Me: 'Thanks for telling me about that, we'll come back to it later. I'd like to ask you about something else. What's your best thing, what do you like doing best?'

He says it's sport of all kinds. I ask him to tell me about it, he says he's good at rugby, and I ask him what it is about him that makes him successful. In conversation he says he's fit and fast, he can stand back to see the pattern of play and react quickly when he needs to. He says he does the same when he's boxing. We talk about his strengths of being both strategic and explosive in sport, and knowing when to do what.

Me: 'Let's go back to the reason that we're meeting today, about your staying in school. Tell me about a time when you could have had a fight ... everything was going that way ... and you didn't. You chose to be strategic rather than explosive.'

He thinks about it, and then he tells me about such a time, in detail. He says his friend accidently damaged something in his home which made him very angry. He said he felt like hitting his friend but instead he just walked back to school with his friend following along behind, and he ignored his friend for the rest of the day.

Me: 'So you're a person who can get near to having a fight, get angry, everything was going that way ... and you can just walk away from it. Is that right?'

Owen: 'Yes.'

Me: 'How come you could do that?'

Owen: 'I thought if I hit him, something else would get broken and then my mum would be mad at me again, so I just walked straight out and back to school.'

Me: 'So if someone asked me about you, like 'what do you know about Owen?', I could tell them 'he's a person who can get angry about something and just walk away'. Is that right?'

Owen: 'Well, it was then.'

Me: 'Yes, that's what I mean, then.'

We talked more about the strengths and resources he showed at the time of this response and about his hopes for the future. In closing the meeting I offered him a task, to notice things going well, wherever they might be happening, and told him I'd meet him in a week to ask him about what he'd noticed. Over the next weeks Owen told me about his success in school and outside in making choices about his behaviour, and we agreed to close our work after five weekly meetings.

What happened next? I checked out Owen's progress when I was in the school later in the year. Owen never had another fight in school since we met for the first time, he completed his exams and stayed out of trouble. After he left, he applied to join the Army as a recruit and was accepted.

What had changed Owen's behaviour, and brought his hopes to reality? Owen had made the vital change himself, with no punishments or rewards, no advice and no guidance in the course of the brief work we did together. In place of external control and exercise of authority that had gone before, we had set up an inquiry, with Owen placed to be the agent in his own change and subsequent success. School systems were unchanged, the work was carried out solely by Owen and myself and school management had to do no more than respond positively to his improvement.

This is a practical illustration of solution-support in a real and critical situation, the solution-focused approach to changing behaviour in schools. It is the subject of this book.

Learning about behaviour

This book is for you, as a beginning teacher. I have written it to provide you with a quiet space for thinking about behaviour, an opportunity to stand back from the action, to reflect on what behaviour is, what can be done about it and why we do what we do, as teachers. I am offering you a fresh perspective and a new approach to changing behaviour in schools, for you to build into your professional practice in a way that makes sense to you, at this creative time in your career. As a working teacher, you need something highly practical that works 'out of the box', that is simple and you can make use of immediately. Solution-support is an approach rooted in practice rather than in theory. The approach was developed by looking carefully for what worked in solving complex behaviour problems, a product of practice-based evidence.

I trained as a teacher in 1994. Before I started my Postgraduate Certificate in Education (PGCE) I had worked with people with complex behaviour difficulties for 15 years. Other people on my course also brought a great deal of similar experiences. A group of us signed up for an optional special educational needs course, expecting to learn something new, to take with us into our classrooms. We were disappointed that, while learning difficulties were covered, there was no mention of behaviour. In my practice schools and as a beginning teacher, I simply had to do my best, based on my experience and on what I could find to read. It was clear that the use of praise, reward and punishment was the unchallenged approach to behaviour management in schools, and as a teacher I had to follow schools' behaviour policies in the best way I could.

Since those days it seems that nothing much has changed. In 2010, the then *Times Educational Supplement*'s behaviour expert, now the current government's new behaviour tsar for the minister of education, advised new teachers that, while most students in a class will comply and behave, 'the few pupils who are kicking off need to be detained, punished, talked to and isolated' (Bennett, 2010). In 2013, the UK government's guidance on improving initial teacher training for behaviour neatly summed up the status quo. It said that trainees must know about generic behaviour management, its systems and techniques, to manage behaviour confidently and with authority. How these systems and techniques were to be used was entirely up to the individual teacher. It emphasized that trainees should be taught to move around the room and look students in the eye, to stamp their authoritative presence on the class. It went down the well-trodden path of reward and punishment, authority and control, the exercise of discipline, by teachers, on students. In the last two lines of the reiteration of traditional wisdom, in a short section on theoretical knowledge, was a glimpse of another world. It stated that trainees should know about scientific research and developments, and how these could be applied to understanding, managing and changing behaviour (DfE, 2012). This book may help you to take up this invitation for change.

Over the last two decades a great deal of research and development on behaviour has taken place, but being largely in fields other than education, it has not been made much use of by those who control and regulate schools and schooling or by teachers in classrooms. Still working in the old way, students continue to be rewarded, controlled and punished, and some, like Owen with his unwanted behaviour, still struggle to make a success of school.

As a teacher in mainstream and special schools and a pupil referral unit, and later as a behaviour support teacher, I had first-hand evidence of the limitations of reward and punishment in changing students' behaviour, and in preventing their marginalization. I was looking for an alternative, and with the combination of good luck and persistence I found what I was looking for – a product of research and development and of a type not envisaged by the established behaviour experts.

From problems to solutions

Twenty years before I started looking, others were investigating a new approach to the problems that people encountered, and it turned out to be just what I was hoping for. In 2000, I attended a compulsory training day for my service on the solution-focused approach to behaviour, delivered in a rural village hall. I did not know of it before and what I heard and saw there struck a chord with me.

In everyday life, having hopes and dreams and achievable plans to make them come true, being optimistic and active is a natural orientation for many people, and is at the heart of solution-support. Bringing this kind of thinking as a structured approach to behaviour in school meant more than an adjustment to the conventional approach to behaviour; it was a paradigm shift in its true sense and it was to lead me to somewhere new.

I applied for a four-day training course, found external funding and set off down a new path.

Returning to work after the training, with the course notes in my hand, I took the solution-focused approach into my work. Keeping the focus on students' resources, success and hopefulness and staying strictly within the boundaries of the approach produced greatly improved outcomes. To put it simply, students' behaviour changed predictably and often quickly. It centred my practice on my skills as a teacher, rather than stretching me to try to be a universal expert on other peoples' behaviour. I began to feel confident that, with this approach, I could make a difference.

I trained other teachers, and a few of us began meeting regularly to reflect on our work, to share successes and stresses, and to plan developments.

As a way of teaching for behaviour change, we became progressively more confident that solution-support addresses the complex and varied needs of students as they meet and overcome difficulties.

REFLECTION

The story at the opening of this chapter is about my work with a student experiencing difficulty in school. This story and others that appear through-out the book are practice-based evidence which gives an insight into a specific practice and the possibility of a form of generalization from one context and one practitioner to another. Simons et al. (2003) call this 'situated generalization', distinguishing it from the type of broad generalization that is commonly understood to relate to evidence-based practice.

Stories of practice should not be pushed aside as mere anecdotes because of their subjectivity, but treated as valuable material in an area notoriously difficult to research. This is particularly important to us as teachers, who share our experiences of practice as stories, and we draw meanings from it. As a form of research it is no less valuable than positivist scientific research, with its controlled trials and large sample sizes.

I hope these stories will resonate with your experience of teaching, and bring you closer to understanding the solutions-focused approach to chang-ing behaviour. Read them reflectively, and look out for what catches your curiosity – an important principle in solution-focused work. Draw out your own meanings as you meet the students in the stories. In the final chapter you will find a simple description of the structure for you to take away with you into your classroom.

Standing in the classroom, feeling calm

There is a great deal of advice and guidance available on how to manage behaviour, and the experts agree on the most important strategies. Established writers acknowledge the importance of the teacher having a positive outlook, and the effect this has on students' behaviour and on their own health and happiness (Rogers, 2011). The solution-focused approach is briefly mentioned in some books (Roffey, 2011) as a tool used in problem-focused behaviour management, but the differences in approach and outcomes of problem-focused and solution-focused teaching are rarely discussed. Many books are packed with quick, easy and effective techniques for teachers to use. Somehow you have to sort out what is right for you in your context. Which approach and strategies match up with your view of yourself as a beginning teacher, with multiple roles to fulfil inside and outside the classroom?

This book will help you to answer this question to the benefit of your practice and your students. As a teacher, you are expected to be a trusted leader with good working relationships with students, to provide help and support when it is needed. As a classroom manager, with systems and procedures you make the classroom run smoothly. As a problem-solver, and in the way you deal with successes and setbacks, you provide an ethical model for students to follow. As a curriculum manager, you make pedagogical choices to match your teaching with the learning task. The way you approach all these aspects of your work, the questions you raise about your practice and the answers you come up with affect the behaviour of students.

REFLECTION

- What do you mean by classroom management?
- What do you mean by behaviour? What do you believe you should do about it?

Good teaching for good behaviour

Thinking about our own beliefs and their importance can give us an insight into the beliefs and values that other people hold about behaviour, and how they perceive these should be handled. This is worthwhile because it affects our own development as teachers interested in behaviour and making decisions about our own practice. For example Sir Michael Wilshaw, the Chief Inspector of Schools in England, said recently in talking about behaviour that 'It's not rocket science' (*Guardian*, 2014), and he sketched a picture of what should be done about it, stating that head teachers are too soft on unruly pupils and that schools should deal with unruliness by coming down hard on the perpetrators. What can you say about the values and beliefs that underpin these comments? Does this mindset match your own?

When I started teaching I had to assume that I knew enough to get by as far as behaviour was concerned. I started as a secondary science teacher and just had to get on with teaching my subject and managing behaviour as best I could. When I started teaching, as a supply teacher, behaviour was an issue from my first minutes in class. The students did not know me, they just saw me as one in a long line of passing faces – supply teachers here for the week and gone on Friday. I was trying to get thirty 13-year-old students to answer the register and they had a well-developed routine for having fun with temporary teachers. What were my beliefs and values when it came to dealing with their behaviour? What was I going to do about behaviour and discipline and building a relationship with these students who were promptly answering the register in other people's names every morning?

Standing at the front

Standing at the front of the class, keeping your breathing steady and looking out on the eager faces looking back at you; what do you know about the students, even before you get to talk to them? You can think whatever you want, and it might be this: most students in the room are having a good time, and are happy enough getting on with learning and growing up. They know what it takes to be a school student and are doing their best to match up to it. Most of the time you will get on well with them, their learning and the behaviour that supports learning seamlessly integrated.

There may be one or two students who disrupt the smooth running of your classroom, but you know they are doing their best too, it is just that sometimes things happen to push them off-course. Think about your own mindset. Do you believe that they are all trying to get it right and some make mistakes? Or do you believe that some are doing their best and some their worst? Does it matter what you believe to be true? It turns out that it does matter, and it makes a big difference to outcomes.

Low-level disruption has a negative effect on learning and it drains the energy of teachers, simultaneously trying to deal with it and teach to a high level. Ofsted (2014) described low-level disruptive behaviour as chatting, calling out, being slow to start, showing a lack of respect and not bringing the right equipment. In primary schools 33–50 per cent of teachers said calling out, disturbing other children and fidgeting with equipment were the main types of disruptive behaviour. In secondary schools 25–33 per cent of teachers reported not getting on with the work, not having the correct equipment and using mobile phones as the main issues. Of the teachers surveyed, 33 per cent reported that they had received no training in managing the behaviour of disruptive students. There is no comment on the type and extent of training received by the remaining 66 per cent.

Most of the issues reported by Ofsted (2014) relate to the management of the classroom. When a teacher develops clear classroom procedures reduced to a few simple rules, it opens the pathway to good classroom management. The issues of respect and relationships are different, in that they cannot be determined by rules; they are affected by the style of leadership the teacher adopts, springing from their beliefs and values. Most students are reassured by the predictability and sense of belonging they associate with a well-managed classroom, and some may need to be reminded of the rules from time to time. A very small number need something more, and push the boundaries more strongly. What do you do for these few? Do they need more control and regulation or something different?

Where do you start?

Even before you enter your classroom you will have a lot of things in mind that you have to do, including maintaining a productive atmosphere and preventing disruption. You have to make a plan. Where is the best place to start?

Marzano et al. (2003) confirmed the commonly held view that successful teaching stands on a foundation of good classroom management. Four principal factors emerged as particularly significant in preventing disruption in class:

1. The mental set of the teacher
2. Disciplinary interventions
3. Teacher–student relationships
4. Rules and procedures

In view of its relative importance, it makes sense to start with the factor of mental set. A teacher's values and beliefs form the building blocks of their practice and have a major effect in producing good classroom behaviour.

Behaviour management – a forced choice or an informed decision?

Consider the following questions:

What beliefs and values held by a teacher prevent disruptive behaviour?

What are your own beliefs and values?

Do you believe that you should exercise authority and use your superior position to control students?

Is it important to you to empathize with students struggling towards understanding?

Do you believe that you should always look on the bright side of life?

Do you believe that being a pessimist is best because then you are never disappointed?

As a teacher it is your values and beliefs that go towards constructing your mental sets and power your practice. Your mental set establishes your default response to a particular type of problem, for example a behaviour problem. It enables you to react automatically to events, and saves you from having to make a thought-out decision. It is thinking habit. How do you decide what to do?

As a beginning teacher, you have to decide what approach you are going to take to the behaviour of students in your classroom. It is not a totally free choice because there will be outside factors to consider, such as the school's organizational approach and behaviour policy, but within these constraints you are free to act professionally. You will have your own more or less well-developed beliefs about behaviour, what it is and how you should approach it, built up over time through your own personal experience. These beliefs go to form your personal mental set on behaviour, but is your general experience the best basis of your professional practice in your role as a teacher? To make a rational choice about whether to rethink your mental set, you need good information on what are the likely outcomes of taking different approaches to classroom behaviour.

What do you think happens if the teacher is too hard or too soft, or just right? The approach a teacher takes to behaviour is largely down to personal choice at the start and becomes strengthened over time as mental sets, or habits, become more established. The approach a whole school takes is similarly largely rooted in habit. Although there is a great deal of information available about the various educational and social effects of rigid control on the one hand or an over lax approach on the other, a school's organizational habits may be sufficiently embedded to resist argument and change. This may also be true of the individual teacher's habits of mind.

In place of balanced individual and organizational judgement, there is a long-running public contest between committed professionals, arguing from their set positions. Those with the traditional control-and-authority mindset may claim that children are spoilt by those with an empathize-and-nurture mindset, but where is the evidence to support the claim and to justify any change of mind, and of mindset, if necessary?

Mental sets for better or for worse

An advantage conferred by having a mental set is that it can make solving a particular type of problem easy and fast. The disadvantage is that if a problem gets assigned to the wrong set, this can interfere with the process of problem-solving to the extent of making the same wrong solution reoccur, or even make the solution impossible to find. People commonly react to problems of a particular type in a particular way, without determining if it is the best approach or even if it will work at all. It is clear that mental sets are more than neutral problem-solving tools, because the nature of the set, as well as its existence, is significant.

Dweck's book *Mindset* (2006) has helped to bring the concept of mental set or mindset, to public attention. From her research, she concluded that people have either a fixed mindset or a growth mindset and can be taught to shift from one to the other. Mindsets exist in the mind as virtual objects, they are the product of imagination, and in the same way you can change your mind, you can change your mindset.

A teacher with a fixed mindset sees behaviour problems as barriers and students as having limited resources and in need of external discipline and external motivation to change. A teacher with a growth mindset sees the same problems as challenges, where change is possible rather than fixed barriers; students are seen as having innate self-motivated potential for learning and growth. Both teacher and student can change their mindset, and students will model their beliefs and their related behaviour on those of their teacher.

Students with the growth mindset respond to difficulties by increasing their effort to overcome them, and enjoy the experience of the challenge rather than giving up or avoiding them as a student with a fixed mindset would do. What sort of mindset do we hope your students will develop?

Up until now the decision as to whether to go for compliance by controlling students with a rod of iron, external discipline and authority or take the different approach of quiet empathy and trust in students' self-motivation to improve has been made purely on the basis of existing mindset or habit. At first sight, we expect students to have a growth mindset to be able to respond to our action as teachers with a fixed mindset if we take the traditional authoritarian approach to behaviour, a paradox that this book will explore.

Teaching for success

The exclusion of students is carried out as part of a strategic behaviour management process. It was estimated in 1998 in the UK that about 100,000 students had fixed-term exclusions and 13,000 were permanently excluded (Social Exclusion Unit, 1998). The most recent figures available are for 2011/12, when about 300,000 fixed-term exclusions were reported, internal unofficial and informal exclusions not included. More than 5,000 students were reported as being permanently excluded annually in recent years. More precisely fixed-term exclusions were 324,110 in 2010/11 and 304,370 in 2011/12; permanent exclusions were 5,080 in 2010/11 and 5,170 in 2011/12 (DfE, 2013).

In the face of these huge numbers, the educational justification for exclusion is very unclear. It does not meet the accepted behaviourist quality criterion of consistent and immediate punishment of students if the intended purpose is to change behaviour, and the learning outcomes of exclusion of all types are commonly not assessed. It does remove a student from their peer group and, theoretically, this deprivation could cause a change in attitude of the student, but then so could a weekend or a school holiday on the same grounds. Many schools have turned to internal exclusion, which is equally hard to justify in educational terms.

Exclusion is also a bureaucratic, procedural matter, as repeated fixed-term exclusions are usually a prerequisite for justifying permanent exclusion, except in the most serious cases. Permanent exclusion is often justified on the grounds that a student is adversely affecting the learning of others. Permanent exclusion of a demanding student may well solve a problem for a school and be in line with their behaviour policy, but there are losses as well as gains. Many students permanently excluded from school experience serious difficulties in their later lives (Powis et al., 1998). There is also a financial penalty, as excluded students are significantly over-represented in prison: in 2015, a place in a young offender's institution in the UK costs about £65,000 a year. Exclusion might seem to solve one problem but it leads to others, merely shifting responsibility for managing behaviour from one agency to another.

Defining behaviour

In education, 'behaviour' usually means bad behaviour, as in 'His learning is OK, it's his behaviour that lets him down'. Behaviour management has come to mean the application of strategies designed to make students learn that the consequence of their bad behaviour is punishment, and that by changing their behaviour they can avoid the unpleasant punishment. In this sense, punishment is seen as the means of teaching good behaviour.

Punishment is a psychological concept, arising from operant conditioning theory, and imported into education in the twentieth century. The role of punishment in bringing about behaviour change might be clearly understood by psychologists, but it is largely misunderstood by educators. The psychological definition of punishment is 'action taken after a behaviour event', which decreases the likelihood of the behaviour occurring again.

To apply punishment effectively, the behaviour must be described precisely in order to make a causal link between the punishment and the behaviour. Without knowing exactly what the existing behaviour is, it is impossible to assess the effect of punishment on it. Psychology is an experimental science, it is not teaching.

Moving to the educational context, punishment might help in clarifying for students what they should *not* do, because it is designed to be unpleasant, but it does not lead to them *learning* what they should be doing instead. In any case, a behaviour change resulting from punishment is temporary, and the original unwanted behaviour often reappears when the punishment ends.

In the last century B. F. Skinner (1904–1990) developed the concept of behaviour modification in experimental animals, conditioning them with rewards and punishments. He warned that in humans, the short-term behavioural gains resulting from punishment needed to be balanced against the potential long-term adverse consequences, for example aggression and antisocial behaviour.

Today in schools behaviour modification is alive and well, a psychological theory driving educational practice. But *teaching* for behaviour, the pedagogical approach to changing behaviour, is less evident. My work and research, over many years, has been concerned with the use of pedagogy, rather than experimental psychological means, to achieve educational ends, with students making changes in their behaviour as they do in building success in maths or music, by learning something new. I have changed and developed my own practice in using a pedagogical approach to behaviour change, and here I am offering it to you, in the hope that you will do the same.

Evidence from practice

'If you have built castles in the air, your work need not be lost; that is where they should be. Now put the foundations under them.'

Henry David Thoreau (1995 [1854])

Practice-based evidence is at the heart of this book. Evidence comes in different forms that are not directly comparable, and have different strengths and purposes, for example qualitative and quantitative evidence, or evidence from cases or from randomized controlled trials. In this book you will read stories of practice; these are not intended to be analysed as objective evidence, but rather to give you an insight into the solution-focused approach to changing behaviour in action. The constant factors in these stories, to bear in mind as you read them, are:

- students experienced the problem-focused approach before my first meeting with them
- the structure of the solution-focused inquiry was consistent (this point is explained in detail in Chapter 10)
- the solution-support was provided by myself, in every case
- the work did not require any other changes – students taking part in solution-support work were subject to whole school policies as usual; teachers and family members where not required to undertake any specific actions as a part of the work.

My hope is that the examples provided throughout each chapter will resonate with your growing experience and bring you closer to the solution-focused way of working. Read them reflectively, drawing out your own meanings as you relate what you read to your own experiences.

You can make practical use of this evidence as it stands, and get on with practicing solution-support. As your experiences build up, you can make the theoretical connections that you need to bring meaning to what you are doing. As you practice you will become more confident that you can solve a problem without talking about it. Working from practice towards theory is one way of developing confidence in the usefulness of solution-focused thinking and support, when you are facing complex problems of your own or those of students and other people. The theory will contribute to the further development of your practice as you reflect on your experiences of teaching in general and teaching behaviour in particular.

Making connections between practice and theory in education

I have travelled a long way as a teacher, from my first days in a special school to the pages of this book. I made a start by looking into educational research and evidence-based educational practice related to behaviour, studying for a Master's degree in education and an Advanced Diploma in Special Educational Needs, followed by my PhD research.

As a trained natural scientist, I was moving into a different world of subjectivities, and a key influence was my PhD supervisor, Professor Ivor Goodson. Over a lifetime in education, he has been thinking deeply and writing about pedagogy, its apparent rigidity and the possibilities for change. He is unequivocal about the connection between a school student as a person with agency and their learning, saying:

Only if the teacher gives the child access to 'action knowledge' can learning take place. An alternative pedagogy would seek to offer the child such an opportunity whilst transmission pedagogy pre-empts it.

Placing the individual pupil in such a central position in defining the approach to knowledge, there is not only a psychological rationale (which some traditionalists concede) but a logical rationale too. All subject matter begins with an original attempt to solve problems and it is this unitary process of knowledge creation that should be the focus of pedagogy, not the transmission of its differentiated products. (Goodson, 2013)

Goodson et al. (2010) examined the relationship between stories that represent people's learning and their action in the world, confirming the view that interior conversations are at the heart of a teacher's map of learning and understanding of their place in the world, and supporting my use of stories in this book as being useful to you.

Your own interior conversations, drawing your beliefs and values together with your practice, will help you to locate yourself in the world of teaching. I would ask you to bear in mind one question throughout, when you are reading the stories of my practice, and checking out the theoretical linkages I make: 'Does this ring true? This, after all, is the question that lies at the heart of all judgement of evidence and of the truth in the stories we tell.

All the stories in this book are accounts of real events, fictionalized to preserve anonymity where necessary. In any case where identification has been agreed to, I make a note of this in the introduction to the story.

References

Bennett, T. (2010) 'Behaviour: How to deal with challenging pupils'. Available at: http://newteachers.tes.co.uk/content/behaviour-how-deal-challenging-pupils (accessed 10 April 2015).

Department for Education (DfE) (2012) 'Improving teacher training for behaviour'. Available at: www.gov.uk/government/publications/improving-teacher-training-for-behaviour (accessed 10 April 2015).

Department for Education (DfE) (2013) 'Statistics: Exclusions'. Available at: www.gov.uk/government/collections/statistics-exclusions (accessed 10 April 2015).

Dweck, C. S. (2006) *Mindset: The New Psychology of Success*. New York: Random House.

Goodson, I. F. (2013) 'Learning, curriculum and life politics: The selected works of Ivor F. Goodson'. Available at: www.ivorgoodson.com/towards-an-alternative-pedagogy (accessed 10 April 2015).

Goodson, I. F., Biesta, G., Tedder, M. and Adair, N. (2010) *Narrative Learning*. Abingdon: Routledge.

Guardian (2014) 'Headteachers too soft on unruly pupils, says Ofsted chief Sir Michael Wilshaw', 25 September. Available at: www.theguardian.com/education/2014/sep/25/headteachers-too-soft-unruly-pupils-ofsted-chief-sir-michael-wilshaw (accessed 10 April 2015).

Marzano, R. J., Marzano, J. S. and Pickering, D. (2003) *Classroom Management that Works: Research-Based Strategies for Every Teacher*. Alexandria, VA: ASCD.

Ofsted (2014) 'Below the radar: Low-level disruption in the country's classrooms'. Available at: www.gov.uk/government/publications/below-the-radar-low-level-disruption-in-the-countrys-classrooms (accessed 10 April 2015).

Powis, B., Griffiths, P., Gossop, M., Lloyd, C. and Strang, J. (1998) 'Drug use and offending behaviour among young people excluded from school', *Drugs: Education, Prevention and Policy*, 5 (3): 245–56.

Roffey, S. (2011) *The New Teacher's Survival Guide to Behaviour*, 2nd edn. London: SAGE.

Rogers, B. (2011) *Classroom Behaviour*, 3rd edn. London: SAGE.

Simons, H., Kushner, S., Jones, K. and James, D. (2003) 'From evidence-based practice to practice-based evidence: The idea of situated generalization', *Research Papers in Education*, 18 (4): 347–64.

Social Exclusion Unit (1998) *Truancy and Social Exclusion*. London: The Stationery Office.

Thoreau, H. D. (1995 [1854]) *Walden: Or, Life in the Woods*. New York: Dover Publications.

2

WHAT DO WE MEAN BY BEHAVIOUR?

This chapter will give you the opportunity to:

- think about behaviour as an aspect of overall learning to be supported through teaching, rather than as a separate category of problem to be managed

- explore your values and beliefs in how you relate to the subject of behaviour in your practice

Thinking about behaviour

What do you think about the four statements below?

1. Behaviour and learning are one and the same, they do not need to be treated separately in the classroom.

Behaviour and learning are two integrated aspects of growing up, as the child and young person makes sense of their world and expresses their understanding through their performance. The aim of teaching is to change their mind, to increase their store of knowledge and their performance range, and develop and strengthen their positive mindsets.

2. All students are learners doing their best, even though sometimes it might not look like it on the surface.

A student behaving badly is a self-motivated person trying to get it right, making a mistake and needing steady, positive educational leadership and guidance from their teacher, to do more of what already supports their success in school.

3. Classroom management and the pedagogical aspects of teaching are the responsibility of the teacher. Active learning, behaviour and behaviour change are the responsibility of the self-motivated student.

The teacher sets up the best possible environment and relies on the students to make the most of it, to learn and work and enjoy problems as challenges.

4. Some students have needs that lie outside the area of a teacher's professional competence. Referral to other professionals may be in the student's best interest.

Given good classroom management and intelligent teaching and support, a student may still not achieve hoped-for changes to ensure their participation, learning and achievement in class. In that case, it is in the student's best interest to have their needs recognized by their teacher, and additional support called in.

REFLECTION

- What do you agree with and why?
- How does the idea of discipline fit in here?
- Why might it be important to support students' resource of self-motivation when they find something challenging?

What can you do about behaviour?

It is clear that learning is affected by students' behaviour, and teachers have to do their best to minimize any adverse effects. Ofsted (2014) reported that the most common behaviour problem faced by teachers is low-level disruption: calling out, fidgeting and off-task activity in class.

There is overall agreement on the strategies teachers should use to prevent low-level disruption in class, to be found in numerous books on behaviour management. The strategies can be summarized as follows:

1. Engage students early on in the lesson.
2. Help them see the relevance of the learning by making connections to the real world.
3. Make the purpose of the lesson clear by sharing learning objectives.
4. Encourage students' active participation.
5. Ask students questions and get them to evaluate their own learning.

6. Maintain pace and momentum throughout the lesson.
7. Restate the purpose of the lesson and give positive feedback.

What beliefs underpin this approach?

This approach to learning could be summed up as good teaching. The teacher can be seen as the leader of learning, and the students as members of the classroom team, prepared to engage, to put effort into their work and to cooperate when the teacher makes all the necessary plans and connections. Students are self-motivated to participate, reflect and self-evaluate; they are active learners, making use of feedback to refocus their efforts. Good students are assumed to bring these strengths and resources with them into class, the teacher does not have to install them.

In these recommendations there is no mention of practices directed at eliminating or correcting bad behaviour. In principle, if this advice is followed, students will behave in ways that support their learning. In practice it does not always work, because other things can get in the way.

The teacher sets out to manage the classroom as an optimum learning environment. Where one classroom activity requires students to discuss things in groups, another activity might need a managed change to individual, quiet concentration. Changing environments, like moving from the lunch-time break into a phonics lesson, or from home to double maths, makes demands on students in knowing where they are and what is expected of them. The teacher's job is to maintain consistency in procedures and boundaries, and keep things simple so that students are clear about their expectations and responsibilities (Rogers, 2011: 37–9).

Given this type of classroom environment and the teacher's belief in students' capabilities and resources, most students integrate thinking and performance, linking behaviour in the classroom with their learning about geography, friendship, maths and everything else. What if well-prepared consistent classroom management and teaching are not sufficient to produce the kind of behaviour that supports effective teaching and learning? Is it possible to be consistent in one's beliefs and values, relating to the students in the room, or is the jump to a different mindset inevitable when unwanted behaviour appears?

Sir Michael Wilshaw, the current head of Ofsted and Chief Inspector of Schools in England, positioned disruptive behaviour as a serious issue to be corrected by firmness and authority on the part of the teacher (Wilshaw, 2014). He advised schools to 'crack down' on the 'odd individuals, Jack the Lad and Sally Showoff', who 'ruin' the education of well-behaved students, and should not be allowed to 'get away with it'.

REFLECTION

- What was Wilshaw's mindset that produced these comments?
- Which beliefs underpin this characterization of students? Compare this belief system with the one in evidence at the start of this chapter.

The need for external control

Discipline, as it is understood in schools, is seen as a good thing and an acceptable and accessible response to rule-breaking. As I discuss later in this book, there are good reasons for using external discipline as a means of emphasizing boundaries and guiding poor behaviour towards good behaviour, *when the situation is not serious.* If a student runs past you in a walk-only corridor, you would call the student back, preferably by their name if you know it, to remind them about the rule and why it is a good idea to walk. When they start to tell you why they were running, that they were late for lunch or whatever, you would listen attentively and make a comment to show that you understood their motivation, remind them again of the rule, thank them for stopping and listening when you called to them, and send them on their way. You could see this as rule-based error correction, and draw a parallel between the teaching response in this case and what would be done to correct an error in arithmetic or spelling.

Jack and Sally present a more serious case and apparently need external discipline to get them to behave, to stop ruining other people's chances. In his statements Wilshaw (2014) expressed this commonly held belief about the way to teach students like Jack and Sally, who persist in being disruptive even in the best-managed classroom. Must they be treated differently from their cooperative peers, to be punished and controlled in order to learn to behave? What if this does not work?

If external control and authority does not work to stop these disruptive students from misbehaving, and they do not have a recognized disorder which might explain their behaviour in some way, the only option appears to be more firmness, more authority, more punishment. And if they still do not change they move further along the behaviour management pathway, via increasingly severe punishment towards exclusion from school.

When discipline morphs into punishment and is applied *in more serious situations* not only is it ineffectual, it also has unintended consequences for the students in question. The results of exclusion can be positive for classmates and the school in general, and removing the adverse effects on other students' learning may be given as a justification. The damage suffered by students who are permanently excluded and are known to be at high risk of losing their access to a full education is tacitly accepted as being necessary for the benefit of the majority (Gazeley et al., 2013). What can we do, as teachers, with these students?

Paradigm shift

At the start of a class you would not ask one student *why* she was taking her equipment out more slowly than the person next to her. It would not help in getting a prompt start, it is not important to know why and it would divert your attention away from getting started. You could accept what she was doing as good enough and quietly compliment the whole class on following the procedure you had previously spent time and energy establishing, such as 'I'm noticing your prompt start this morning'.

Instead of looking at *what* is going wrong and *why* it went wrong, you might assume she is doing her best and today her best happens to be at a slower pace than usual. Letting the student know that you see her as doing her best, along with the rest of her classmates, helps her to know where she is as a member of the group in your class.

In your training, you may have come across the advice I mentioned earlier to promote good behaviour in class. You may have learned other things like the importance of 'wait time' and 'long enough' for students to respond to a question or an instruction (Rogers, 2006). It is assumed that once teachers know what they should do, they will naturally know how to put the factual knowledge into practice.

However, extensive research has shown that it is possible to change how teachers *think* about their practice, by acquiring new knowledge, without any change coming about in what those teachers actually *do* in the class-room. Two promising approaches to bringing about changes in practice are individual coaching of teachers and forming learning communities (Wiliam 2008). It is a crucial issue for me, because I hope that you will come to *think* differently about behaviour through reading this book and that your *practice* will change. I will come back to these issues of coaching and communities in the last chapter of this book.

Cause and effect

We have a strong tendency to ask a student *why* they behaved in a particular way when something goes wrong in setting out the project of changing their behaviour. It is an expression of the cause/effect science that seeks to establish the cause of behaviour and then we can suggest ways of changing it. If you see one boy attack another in the playground it is natural to call him over and ask him why he did it, assuming that the student knows *why*. In my experience they do not know why, although they might try to help you by guessing. It does not get you very far.

If you need to, test it out on yourself. When you behave in an out-of-character way, ask yourself '*Why* did I do *that?*'– I guarantee you will not come up with a simple answer. You will always find several inter-related factors that affect your behaviour when you start looking for them, and it is similar for students in school except that their search skills may not be as well-developed as yours. Faced with a complex behaviour problem, it is rarely possible to connect cause and effect in trying to solve it. Behaviour can be tracked to a whole range of possible causes, some of them might be known to the person behaving in a certain way and some not, all of them interconnected and uncertain.

REFLECTION

- What is the appropriate teaching approach when there is this degree of uncertainty about the intended learning goals?

- What kind of teaching can visualize an appropriate goal and track progress towards it, at the same time as enabling new learning?

- What mindset underpins your thinking about pedagogy?

The key lies in the questions. When we replace directions with questions we are setting up an inquiry. As with any pedagogical approach, inquiry needs to be structured. Solution-support provides a simple and consistent structure for the inquiry. My aim is to give you enough information to confirm your present mindset or to make the change and provide you with enough support to enable you to put your thinking into practice, as Wiliam (2008) suggested.

Inquiry?

It is not within the scope of this book to examine pedagogy in great detail. There are also major questions relating to pedagogy, like whether learning is a biological function (nature) or an environmental one (nurture), which we will pass by. Briefly, if you look at direct instruction (Engelmann and Carnine, 1991) at one end of the pedagogical spectrum, in its pure form it is based on a script that delivers faultless instruction. Misinterpretation of the faultless instruction means that the learner must be faulty, the fault must be determined through behaviour analysis, and corrected by a remedial programme. This type of instruction is in the form of a scientific experiment, and since the learner is an uncontrollable variable and the instruction is controlled and held constant, failure of instruction must be caused by learner variability. Direct instruction has been shown to produce good results when it is used to teach basic skills. While Engelmann and Carnine's (1991) form of direct instruction has appeared in schools in the UK and the USA, notably in the teaching of basic skills in primary school, teacher-centred instruction is in widespread use and is valuable where accurate knowledge reproduction is the intended outcome of teaching.

At the other end of the pedagogical spectrum is inquiry, a learner-centred approach where growth in the autonomy of the student is an intended outcome, with their development of creative problem-solving and thinking skills. Inquiry can be carried out at different levels, as the teacher facilitates the progressive deployment of students' autonomy with varying degrees of guidance (Banchi and Bell, 2008). Applying this to the teacher's pedagogical approach to students' learning about behaviour, and moving from directing to inquiring, means entering a different reality. The teacher-controlled, scripted objectivity of a behaviour policy's sanctions or punishments is replaced by the intentional uncertainty of open inquiry, where the student is at the centre as an active agent and the teacher facilitates the inquiry.

Within education in general there has been a long-term contest between the proponents of the teacher-centred directive approach and those who support student-centred inquiry, continuing the older traditional/progressive argument. But there has been no such contest in the field of behaviour. Schools in the UK and elsewhere adopted the findings of the earliest psychologists of learning, the behaviourists, and adopted their experimental procedures. The directive behaviourist approach has ruled unchallenged until now. So what has changed?

Refocusing from problems to solutions – making the change

In some ways, education and psychotherapy have shared interests in that they are both concerned with personal learning and change and both are strongly influenced by scientific findings, particularly those of psychologists. Psychotherapy as a discipline has always mentioned goals such as personality reconstruction and behaviour modification, but has devoted its thinking, study and research efforts to the problems rather than the solutions that people have brought to therapy. This remained the case until the 1980s when new thinking, along radically different lines, began to open up new possibilities.

Steve de Shazer was working as a family therapist through the 1980s when constructivism was making an impact, as an alternative approach to understanding how people make sense of the world. As a constructivist, de Shazer (1988) argued that people generate knowledge and meaning from an interaction between their experiences and their ideas. Meaning is a product of people's thinking.

This conception can be contrasted with objectivism, which is based on the argument that knowledge and meaning exist in the world as realities, regardless of an individual person and their experiences. Meaning is not the product of peoples' thinking, rather it has an independent existence.

De Shazer reinterpreted psychotherapy in constructivist terms, and came to some surprising conclusions that he tested out in his practical family therapy work, helping people to make changes in their lives through their behaviour. From the continuous cycle of reflection and practice, solution-focused brief therapy (SFBT) was developed. When I first came across this approach, as a teacher, it clearly offered a new way to think about changing behaviour in schools, but could it be interpreted as pedagogical, rather than therapeutic, work? Both are designed to support change and solve problems, so that seemed like the place to look for connections, in the area of solution-focused problem solving.

From the solution-focused perspective, a problem can only exist where there is the possibility of it being solved. When the solution is achieved, the problem disappears. A problem with no solution is not a problem, it is a fact-of-life, part of the largely unchanging scenery that forms the backdrop to our lives (de Shazer, 1988: 6–9). This is in stark contrast to the thinking behind conventional, problem-focused behaviour management. From this perspective problems exist regardless of whether a solution can be found; the nature of a problem determines its solution and getting to understand the problem is the first step towards solving it.

To this problem-focused way of thinking, a behaviour problem is a concrete thing that has an independent existence; it can be described, and if the right steps are taken it can be eliminated. The practical solution-focused approach to behaviour change makes different starting assumptions: that solutions and problems are not objective concrete things, rather they are constructed by people. The solution is no more determined by the problem than the problem is by the solution, and they only exist relative to one another, and once the solution is present that which was previously a problem becomes just a part of ordinary life.

For example, when students come into class and sit down in the correct seats ready to start work, you do not recognize this as the solution to the problem of not coming into class properly and sitting in the wrong seats. You do not assume there is a problem and wait with bated breath to see what goes wrong.

You do not need to pay attention to a potential problem every time it might happen; students generally carry out the procedures independently without the need for external motivation. However, if one class group does not come in quietly and settle down, your attention would be drawn to it, you would identify the problem, spend some time teaching them the procedure and talking to them about why it is a good idea. After a few reminders, with the procedure in place and the solution in action, the problem disappears and you have your attention freed up for other things.

I am a trained scientist, and I had been doing problem-focused problem solving for 25 years before I came into teaching. When I started working in this different, solution-focused way I had to pay close attention to staying within the paradigm, to avoid going back to problem-focused working. Solution-focused working requires a shift in thinking, and support for putting it into practice. The solution is the key, investigating the nature of the problem is unnecessary. Working directly towards the solution eliminates the need to take the long route, via problem description and analysis as well as having other important beneficial outcomes (explained later in Chapter 7, on praise and reward). Importantly for teachers, solution-support helps a student to put their knowledge to creative use, to make their own changes where the problem-focused management approach, intended to motivate them externally, fails to do so.

As a teacher, are you obliged to manage students' behaviour?

Most of the students in any group will cooperate with you, laugh or groan at your jokes and surprise you with their amazing and amusing ideas. At the start of your teaching day, it is natural for you to hope it will go well, and you see students as a resourceful, successful, hopeful group of people. You trust them to do their best to stay with you when you forge ahead, and forgive you when you stumble. You know they too hope to be at their best as the day begins, even when it does not quite work out that way, and they recognize the same hope in you. There will be times when, despite your best hopes and plans, things go awry, but together with your co-operative students you will bounce back to regain the usual good-natured productivity of your classroom.

In the class group it is likely that a few students will do things differently, will shout out the right answers in the wrong places, and interrupt you and their fellow students. If this happens, should you characterize them differently from the happy cooperators in the room in order to fulfil your professional responsibilities as leader and manager? Are they doing their best as resourceful, hopeful successful people and falling short? Or are they really doing their worst, intentionally making your life more difficult? Do you need to exert more control, to regulate and punish them to stop them behaving badly? Or is it possible to work directly towards the solution within your remit as a teacher? Does the change students need to make have to come from outside, through your behaviour management skills, or can it come from inside, through students' strengths of resourcefulness, hopefulness and successful achievement?

Doing what comes naturally

It might seem natural to manage behaviour in the classroom through control and regulation, because this way of working is so well established. Certainly, in planning and putting into place your classroom management procedures, the discipline aspects of classroom management that I mentioned earlier, the teacher exerts a necessary degree of control. If a student does not appear to have self-control, like Owen whom you met in Chapter 1, then it might seem obvious that he must be controlled by someone else, the teacher acting as the behaviour manager. But if we know our mindset, we can keep a clear head and continue to see them as resourceful, successful and hopeful, even when the evidence of their apparently uncontrolled behaviour is telling us otherwise, surprising things happen.

Clearly, there will be students who seem to be resistant and uncooperative, as Owen seemed to be. In the solution-focused way of standing things on their head, we see resistance as a person's best attempt at cooperation, something to be curious about and a hint to ask a different question. By approaching people as successful and hopeful it becomes more likely that their resources will be strengthened and they will succeed as we saw with Owen. I will talk about this in more detail in Chapter 7. To take this approach as a teacher you need a framework of ideas to provide structure, and solution-support provides such a framework.

More work – why bother?

If building a new mental set and developing a new practice means more work for you, why bother?

Because it makes a difference, and that is the reason that many of us come into teaching. If a student is struggling, we want to do something to make a difference, leading to better outcomes.

It is possible to see someone as doing their best, even when on the surface it looks as if they are doing their worst, and their worst is what other people might tell you about them. Students might even say it about themselves. But when you yourself are at your best, your new perspective can help you to focus on their resources and strengths and successes, to enable them in turn to be at their best, doing their best.

In addition to the outwardly disruptive students, there are others for whom solution-support is well suited; those whom you hardly notice, who do not speak or smile much, who do not make demands and quietly under-achieve. They may be overlooked just because they are undemanding, and teachers' energies are taken up with other louder personalities. What might happen if your belief system, your mental set, characterized them as hopeful, successful and resourceful too? Would that make a difference?

A teacher's task is to enable all students to be successful learners, without the loudest getting all the attention or the quietest getting lost in the noise. In my experience, being able to draw on solution-support is a useful resource, as a thoughtful alternative to problem-focused work. It gives another perspective on behaviour of all kinds and on what we mean when we consider changing behaviour.

Better handwriting for better behaviour

In traditional behaviour management terms, it is accepted that a solution to a problem must have a logical relationship to the problem itself. If the problem is that a student frequently shouts at his teachers and runs out of class, we have to stop him doing it, and punishing him might seem all we have to make him change. It seems logical. But if we asked the student what they thought might be useful in bringing about a change, what might they say? Probably not that they should be punished. Of course, they are not experts in behaviour and they might come up with something that seems completely irrelevant, which might make absolutely no sense to you but, mysteriously, makes sense to them. For the solution to a behaviour problem to be effective, it must relate to the student's conception of what needs to change, and in solution-focused work we consult the expert on the student: the student themselves.

REFLECTION

As you read the following story, think about the connection between the problem and the solution. Make notes about what catches your interest. Relate it to your growing understanding of solution-support.

Ask the expert

I was asked to work with a 13-year-old boy in mainstream school. The referral notes told me he frequently swore at teachers, and would run out of class and around the school. The school behaviour policy had been followed, and all the usual efforts had been made to stop him being disruptive. His mother had been called in to school several times as his behaviour worsened. He had been temporarily excluded but still showed no improvement, and the only remaining step was permanent exclusion, which was imminent.

I met him and his mother in school in a small meeting room, opposite the Deputy Head's office. I explained that I was interested in looking forward rather than backward, and at what was working rather than at what had gone wrong. The boy's mother said that was a relief, because every time she came into school it was to talk about the trouble he had caused, and it did not seem to get them anywhere.

I said I had been called in to school because of the high risk of the student's permanent exclusion. My job was to do something useful to prevent that from happening, and it was work I did with students of all ages, in different schools. We talked for a few minutes about permanent exclusion, because the student was not clear about it.

I asked the student what would be useful for us to work on, for things to go better in school. He suggested 'My behaviour?' and we agreed on that. Then we talked about his successes, his strengths and resources, what he liked doing and what he was good at, for 15 minutes. Then I said:

Me: Let's get back to the project, your behaviour. What might you do a bit differently for things to go better in school?

Student: Improve my handwriting?

I drew a 1 to 10 scale for 'handwriting' in my notebook, with 1 as just before we met and 10 for where we hoped to be in a month's time. I asked him to mark his current position and where he hoped to be two weeks. He marked the scale at 3 and 5.

Me: Suppose your handwriting improves, and you're moving a bit towards 5, what would be happening to move you there?

He said he would be having three 20-minute handwriting sessions every week with the special educational needs coordinator (SENCO).

I asked him to mark a 1–10 confidence scale, with 10 'confident my behaviour will be better when my handwriting is better' and 1 'not confident'. He marked the scale at 10.

Me: You'd like the SENCO to help you, but I can't make that happen because I am not her boss. I can ask her if it's possible, so if you could wait here for me for a few minutes with your Mum I'll go and do that. Is that OK?

They both agreed it would be.
I returned after a few minutes.

Me: The SENCO says she'd be pleased to help you. She would like to know when you want to start work.

Student: Tomorrow?

Me: OK, I'll tell her when we've finished here, and she said she will let you know when and where to meet her. Is there anything else you need?

Student: No.

Me: There are just two things to do before we end today, to share compliments and to give you a task. I'm going to ask your mum to give you a compliment, I am going to do that too and I'm going to ask you to compliment yourself about today. Who would you like to go first?

Student: Mum.

We shared compliments.

Me: Now the last thing – your task. I'd like to ask you to notice what's going well. When we meet next time I will ask you about that. I'll say 'what have you noticed that's gone well since the last time we met?' OK?

He was right about the handwriting. When we met next, he'd noticed a lot of things going well for him. He'd stopped swearing and running. He did his extra handwriting lessons. He was never excluded again. His Mum said he seemed more confident and happier in general, and she said he was helping her more around the house without being asked.

We finished our work after five meetings of about half an hour for the first, and 15 minutes in follow-up sessions. At the final review meeting he showed me his handwriting and told me he was happy with it. As I walked away from that first meeting, I remember clearly walking out of the school, shaking my head and laughing in wonder. What an unlikely connection.

And what happened to this student subsequently? He maintained his place and left school at 16.

COMMENT

A key idea in solutions-focused thinking and solution-support is that the student is the expert on themselves, and this point is confirmed in the above story. He knew what the solution was, I did not need to guess, I simply asked him. That it seemed an unlikely connection to me was irrelevant. I checked it out with him, and he felt confident that improving his handwriting would make the difference. It turned out that he was right.

What do you notice about motivation here? There was no external praise or reward. I asked him to notice his successes and we talked about them. He carried through his programme of handwriting improvement to his satisfaction. Was it hard for him to make this change? I have no idea. Did it make people happier? It seemed to. Steve de Shazer (1988) said that the nature of a problem does not determine its solution. It is more productive to ignore the problem and use the time available to find the solution, rather than in trying to invent a theory which would explain the problem logically, and maybe get it wrong.

Teaching, guidance, counselling and a meeting of minds

As a teacher you expect to act as a counsellor, coach and guide in your pastoral work with students. This aspect of the work was addressed in the Elton Report on Discipline in schools (DoES and the Welsh Office, 1989), which proposed that teachers should receive counselling training in line with a more child-centred approach to behaviour. Solution-focused support has been repeatedly suggested as a useful approach since then. Hill (1999) included solution-focused counselling as a new development in his review of effective support as particularly suited to the teacher's pastoral role. Ajmal and Rees published *Solutions in Schools* in 2001 and most recently Ratner and Yusuf (2015) have written a new book on solution-focused coaching in schools. How do guidance, counselling and coaching relate to you as a teacher? The terminology is different – teachers do pastoral work while counsellors and therapists provide therapeutic care – but the practices and aims are mutually understandable. School-based professional counsellors provide students with a space to talk and find ways to move forward. A number of counselling models are in use, including solution-focused brief therapy and solution-focused coaching. Why is the solution-focused approach particularly well-matched to the needs of teachers, providing support to students in school? Because in place of diagnosis and expert suggestions as to what should work to change a student's behaviour, we listen out for what is already working and for the practical steps the student knows they can take to get there.

Who needs counselling or coaching?

Cooper (2013) found that two-thirds of students referred to professional school counsellors in the UK were dealing with the kinds of problems that children and young people can expect to meet and solve in the course of growing up, rather than more serious psychological issues. Students in difficulty are referred by class teachers, who apparently feel they do not have the necessary skills to help these students. Teachers with pastoral responsibilities confirm the class teachers' assessments and refer students onward to the professional counsellor. Teachers who have relevant training can provide more effective counselling or coaching at the first level, where solution-support will prove to be effective in many cases. Students with more serious difficulties can be referred by the teacher to the professional counsellor or coach, if available in school. If the student's problems are more serious and fail to be resolved within the counselling or coaching programme, the counsellor, the student's parents or carers may consult their general practitioner (GP), and school staff and school-based health professionals can contribute to a referral via the GP to the child and adolescent mental health services (CAMHS).

In 2008, Wales introduced counselling as an integral part of school provision. It had been shown to:

- complement pastoral care systems
- support teachers' care of children and young people and their management of those with emotional and behavioural difficulties
- offer training to teachers in counselling skills and stress management
- provide consultation, training, support and supervision of strategies to counteract problems such as bullying and truancy
- influence drug and sex education policies within a confidential framework
- contribute to the personal and social education framework curriculum
- support effective child protection procedures.

(Welsh Government, 2011)

In this model counselling is seen as more than a support service for students with the highest level of needs, it also increases capacity in school by supporting and training teachers and supporting whole-school developments (Ratner and Yusuf, 2015). The shift to focusing on solutions and away from controlling and punishing badly behaved students, or treating bad behaviour as an illness requiring medical or psychological treatment, can help to build confidence for teachers and students as successes are realized together.

Solution-support is a safe practice in that: it does not demand specific expertise on the psychological and medical interpretations of behaviour on the part of the teacher, who can confidently do effective work with brief training; it does not focus on problems and possible traumatic events a student might have experienced; if it does nothing else, it reminds students about their strengths, resources and successes and their ability to think for themselves and act independently.

Conclusion

As a beginning teacher you have to pay attention to behaviour and learning whilst establishing the kind of classroom environment you hope for. Acting in your classroom management role you will decide on the structural framework you are going to put in place, the settled scenery and routine procedures that will help things to run smoothly. Some will be given (e.g. general school rules and the curriculum) and some will be under your control. You may be given behaviour management procedures to follow; for example, what to do if you need a student to leave the room, and how to use the school's punishment regime if a student misbehaves.

You know that there is more to teaching than management, and that your relationship with your students has a great influence on outcomes. Your area of direct influence extends from the door to your room, into the physical space of the room and the multidimensional minds of your students. There may be school policy guidelines on the type of relationship the school advocates, and they may emphasize leadership, responsiveness, clarity and other characteriztics that provide the bedrock of good relationships between teachers and students. The practicalities of how you interpret all of this and the way students come to see you, as their teacher, is up to you.

In this chapter I have suggested that how you characterize your students, your mindset, is something for you to reflect upon. If you see them as resourceful, hopeful, successful people, there is a good chance that is how they will be in your thoughtfully constructed environment for learning. When problems do crop up, if you take the solution-focused approach to them you can be consistent in how you characterize the people involved, as resourceful, hopeful and successful, yourself included, when things are going well and when they are going not so well. You may put in place a procedure for a particular aspect of classroom management (e.g. students coming in to the room and settling down to work), but it is not reliably promoting the environment you want in your room.

You have several options for action. You could leave the procedure unchanged and use your control and authority to make students comply. You could focus on the problem, try to figure out what is going wrong and why the procedure does not work, so that you can adjust it and then get the students to comply. Of course, when the teacher exerts control and authority to achieve compliance, students are characterized as dependent, in need of control and failing, promoting the problem-focused mindset.

Or you could take the solution-focused approach: get a clear picture of how things would be when coming into the room and settling down went smoothly, and then find out what is already working. You could undertake the inquiry with the students, modelling an alternative approach to problem solving and coming up with an agreed procedure that, rather than demanding compliance, would encourage cooperation. In Chapter 10 there is a framework for you to use when trying this out for yourself.

If it is a people-problem rather than a management issue where a student is behaving in a way that is disturbing the smooth operation of the class, again you have a choice of options. You could exert control and apply external discipline. If you take the problem-focused behaviour management path, you will be setting up a different relationship to the strengths-based one you had previously been building. If you move straight into the punishment regime, you risk further opposition and non-compliance, and damage to the positive relationship you had before.

Or you could take the solution-focused approach, as I did with the boy who improved his handwriting, characterizing him as resourceful, successful and hopeful when from school reports he was resistant to change and failing in school. You could solve the problem cooperatively, do it through a process of solution-focused inquiry, and strengthen your productive relationship at the same time. How do I know? I have the evidence from my practice, with many students and a whole variety of problems, and it works. 'Changing behaviour' goes further than supporting useful change in the disruptive or withdrawn behaviour of students; it includes our behaviour as teachers and the beliefs that drive our action. Maybe this book should have had a longer title, 'Changing behaviour and changing your mind'.

References

Ajmal, Y., Rees, I. (2001) *Solutions in Schools: Creative Applications of Solution Focused Brief Thinking with Young People and Adults.* London: BT Press.

Banchi, H. and Bell, R. (2008) 'The many levels of inquiry', *Science and Children*, 46 (2): 26–9.

Cooper, M. (2013) 'Counselling in UK secondary schools', *Therapy Today*, 24 (5): 26–8.

de Shazer, S. (1988) *Clues: Investigating Solutions in Brief Therapy.* New York: Norton.

Department of Education and Science and the Welsh Office (1989) *Discipline in Schools: Report of the Committee of Inquiry Chaired by Lord Elton.* London: HMSO.

Engelmann, S. and Carnine, D. (1991) *Theory of Instruction: Principles and Applications*, Eugene, OR: ADI Press.

Gazeley, L., Marrable, T., Brown, C. and Boddy, J. (2013) *Reducing Inequalities in School Exclusion: Learning From Good Practice*. Falmer: University of Sussex.

Hill, M. (1999) *Effective Ways of Working with Children and their Families*. London: Jessica Kingsley.

Ofsted (2014) 'Below the radar: Low-level disruption in the country's classrooms'. Available at: www.gov.uk/government/publications/below-the-radar-low-level-disruption-in-the-countrys-classrooms (accessed 10 April 2015).

Ratner, H. and Yusuf, Y. (2015) *Brief Coaching with Children and Young People: A Solution Focused Approach*. London: Routledge.

Rogers, B. (2006) *Cracking the Hard Class*, 2nd edn. London: SAGE.

Rogers, B. (2011) *Classroom Behaviour*, 3rd edn. London: SAGE.

Welsh Government (2011) 'Evaluation of the Welsh school-based counselling strategy: Final report'. Available at: http://gov.wales/statistics-and-research/evaluation-welsh-school-based-counselling-strategy/?lang=en (accessed 10 April 2015).

Wiliam, D. (2008) 'Changing classroom practice', *Informative Assessment*, 65 (4): 36–42.

Wilshaw, M. (2014) 'Pupils lose an hour of learning "because of bad behaviour"'. Available at: www.itv.com/news/update/2014–09–25/wilshaw-education/ (accessed 10 April 2015).

3

BECOMING THE BEST TEACHER YOU CAN BE

This chapter will give you the opportunity to:

- explore the planning aspect of classroom management
- connect classroom management with solution-focused teaching as part of a planned process
- introduce a pedagogical view of solution-focused teaching and solution-support as a form of inquiry

'I learned this, at least, by my experiment: that if one advances confidently in the direction of his dreams, and endeavours to live the life which he has imagined, he will meet with a success unexpected in common hours.'

Henry David Thoreau, *Walden* (1854)

Planning for success

What issues will you have to deal with in becoming the best teacher you can be? Being a successful teacher depends on both who you are and what you do, and classroom management is high on the list of what you do. When classroom management goes well, it produces the framework for order, adaptability and learning in the classroom. It is practically invisible to an outside observer, and for this reason it is hard for a new teacher to model their own organizing strategies on those of a more experienced colleague. The development work and programme planning that an experienced teacher has done to set up the classroom learning environment in the first days of the school year is largely hidden.

The planning part of classroom management starts before you step into the classroom. An important task is organizing information and advice from multiple sources, such as your teacher training course, from experienced teachers and from books on classroom management and stripping it down to a manageable and ordered plan for action. One way to structure the process is to break it up into initial and active pre-planning, and in-flight and follow-up planning (Freiberg, 2002). Our concern here is the pre-planning phase: initial planning requires imaginative visualization of the teaching and the students' responses to it, whereas active planning specifies the resources needed for the lesson. The two components go to make up a programme with intended outcomes, and putting together intentions, resources and information requires the programme to be planned in some way.

Forward planning, working backwards

When the planning of classroom management is carried out in a structured way it is more likely that the intended outcomes will be achieved, and assessment of the impact of the activity is simplified, giving guidance on what to do next. When you come across a particular aspect of your class-room management to which you need to pay attention, you could treat this as a project to be planned, implemented and reviewed. A project in this sense is a short-term activity with a defined intended outcome, and a clear path from the input of resources to the outcome.

In the world of project management outside of education, but little known within schools, is a well established tool known as logic modelling. This model develops an image of how things will be in the future, when improved outcomes are already in place, and then systematically set out the steps necessary to get there. You state your intended outcome, and work backwards to specify what is needed to realize it (Funnell and Rogers, 2011). The phases of the project are logically connected by 'if/then' state-ments: if we do this activity, then this will be the result. One way of defining a project is by working backwards from a hoped-for future to the present, to decide whether the idea is possible and redesigning it if necessary. Once you have settled on your project, you can write a logic-modelled plan for its implementation.

One aim of this book is to open up the concept of problem-solving, as applied to behaviour in school. Offering the solution-focused approach as a practical alternative to the problem-focused approach is an aspect of this opening up. I have introduced the solution-focused approach to problem solving and solution-support in Chapters 1 and 2, and you may be able to draw parallels between outcome-focused logic modelling and solution-support already, as an aside to the main drive of the book.

I have introduced logic-modelling here as a simple tool to help you to plan your way systematically through the initial and active components (Freiberg, 2002) of classroom management. You may also find it useful for other planning tasks you become involved with in school, such as curriculum and departmental planning.

There are extensive free resources available on the Internet to support your use of logic modelling if you choose to take it up, and I will do no more here than give it this brief recommendation.

REFLECTION

- If you decide to investigate logic modelling, note down three similarities between outcome-focused logic modelling and solution-support.

- Note down five areas of practice where you could visualize an outcome-focused method of planning your classroom management which could be useful to you.

Adopting strategies and developing skills for planning and delivery of classroom management procedures can help to reduce the reliance on trial and error, which depends on getting things wrong in order to put them right. In principle, if your classroom management is successful, there is less need to manage routine classroom behaviour as a separate issue. If things go wrong and energy is drawn into fire-fighting, it is harder for the teacher to keep the pace up and the challenge and interest alive necessary to engage students in active learning and prevent unwanted behaviour happening. If classroom management proves too difficult to plan and put into effect, trying to micro-manage student discipline and disruption can exhaust the teacher. Alternatively, systematic planning and review of classroom management can help the teacher to retain a sense of control and self-efficacy (Freiberg, 2002).

Logic modelling may prove useful to you in systematically planning your classroom management, and this will help to prevent behaviour emerging that is disruptive to learning. When you have confidence in your classroom management, you can plan your response to students' needs when they do not or cannot manage their own behaviour in ways that promote learning. In this way you can plan to provide solution-support as a timely action, to prevent mildly disruptive behaviour from escalating to a point where the school's behaviour policy requirements for sanctions or punishments come into play. Again it is worth recalling that this additional support will only be needed by a very small number of students, and should not risk overloading you with additional work. A planned response can mean that you take on the behaviour work that is appropriate to your teaching role, and where additional external support for a student is needed you have evidence to justify it. If solution-support is not effective, and the review of the work demonstrates this, the student may need additional resources and in the way of support, such as specialist coaching or counselling, or specialist assessment.

Making changes

In my work as a behaviour support teacher, I was routinely called in to school where a specific student was causing problems and the school had used up all its strategies without success. The referral to me often came about as a last-ditch attempt to get a student to alter their behaviour. Consequently I often entered a stuck situation, where a student was habitually breaking the rules and the school was habitually restating and reinforcing the boundaries to no effect. Could something different have been done before things got to this critical situation? When I started work as a behaviour support teacher, I did not know of any alternative to the established approach of getting to grips with the problem, trying to figure out what caused it and then attacking the cause. It often proved impossible to get a full account of the factors underlying a student's behaviour problem and observation in class was the routine first step, with feedback and recommendations to the teacher on classroom management. But teachers often reported that students behaved much better with a stranger in the room, and that we as external specialists did not get to see the real problems. They would also often say that they had already done what we were suggesting. After all, these were experienced teachers working with their students every day in many cases. I started doing something different, to work directly with students using solution-support as the approach.

Solution-support in action: a case story

Andy was in his last few months at primary school. His behaviour had recently seriously deteriorated and he was being disruptive in class. The school staff had tried to talk him to find out what had gone wrong, but he was reluctant to accept help and his behaviour was getting worse. Andy lived in a residential home and had been living in care since he was very young.

I had developed a programme of five brief solution-support meetings over four weeks, the first to set up the work and the last to review progress and decide the next steps. I arranged to meet Andy in school as usual and we met one-to-one throughout. I kept the Deputy Head informed by meeting her for a few minutes after each meeting.

In the five meetings Andy and I talked about his resources, his hopes and the solution to his problem already happening rather than something new and untried. We did not talk about the problem that had prompted the referral because it is not necessary in solution-focused work.

We set about exploring the solutions. An important characteristic of effective solution-focused behaviour support from the perspective of a busy teacher is that it does not demand developed expertise in behaviour and its causes, because the approach is not analytical. Andy himself had the specific expertise that we needed for the project. My role was to be a reliable solution-focused partner and guide in the inquiry.

The solution-focused inquiry

We set up a solution-focused inquiry, my role being to maintain a clear focus on solutions, on successes in the present and best-hopes for the future. I started by asking Andy what would be useful for us to work on. He told me that he was worried about going to high school. This gave us the project, the focus of our inquiry. I asked him to scale his confidence on a 1–10 scale, as it was just before we started talking. He said he was at minus 10.

> *Me*: So just when we started 10 minutes ago you were at minus 10, and how about right now?
>
> *Andy*: Zero.
>
> *Me*: So you've moved from minus 10 to zero in the few minutes since we started. What is it about you that could do that?
>
> *Andy*: I want to be ready to move and ... I'm talking, to you.

I asked him about his best hopes, as expressed on his confidence scale. He said he hoped to be at 10 on the scale by the end of term, eight weeks away. I asked him what he might be doing differently for that to happen. He described it clearly, that he would be doing extra maths lessons and have an English dictionary to use at home. He wanted to have a dictionary of his own to be able to use it when he was in high school. He had never owned one before. I asked him if he would like to go to talk to the Deputy Head with me, to see what we could arrange. We went to her office and organized the extra maths lessons to strengthen the specific areas that he identified. She said she would see if there was any money available for the dictionary. Andy's behaviour changed from the time of our first meeting. In class and in his extra lessons he worked hard, behaved well and his confidence about transition increased, as he had hoped it would.

At our fifth meeting, to review the project, Andy said he was ready to go to high school. I asked him to keep on looking out for what was going well. I checked with him to see if there was anything else he needed. He said he was fine and we ended our work. The work had taken two hours of contact time, spread over a month.

COMMENT

Notice the feedback cycle; formative assessment is built in to the solution-support structure. Take seriously what the student says, as he is doing his best to cooperate. Andy looked at my 1–10 scale (10 ready to go to high school, 1 the opposite of that) carefully. He said in a very matter-of-fact way that he was at minus 10 on the scale at the start. I took that as a clear sign that he was engaged in the work, taking responsibility for the meaning of the scale. I was to look for change already happening, rather than being caught out by him scoring himself way off the end of the scale. This was a hopeful start.

As soon as change towards the best hope can be seen, the material is there to provide feedback and challenge. This is very different to a process directed by the final goal, where intermediate stages are decided by the adult and the student is expected to achieve or fail.

And what about the deteriorating behaviour problem? The fact it was never mentioned is important, because it cannot be a part of the future story that was in Andy's mind, and the mental map of 'being prepared for the change of schools'.

Getting focused

Solution-support provides a future-orientated, structured and reliable way for a teacher to work with a student with any kind of problem in school, including behaviour problems. Solution-support is in the form of an inquiry, constructed around a small number of open questions. It sits comfortably with other procedures in school such as established behaviour management, including disciplinary procedures, because it focuses on the student making the best of the actual situation in school. From the solution-focused perspective a student with behaviour that could be usefully different is characterized as successful, hopeful and self-motivated to change. From the problem-focused perspective the same person would be seen as failing, in deficit and lacking resources and motivation that has to be supplied from the outside. Whether you approach a conversation with a student in difficulties with the solution-focused or the problem-focused mindset is a matter of choice based on a set of beliefs.

Does it make any difference which mindset you adopt?

If a student perceives their teacher seeing them as a successful, hopeful and resourceful person, it becomes more likely that they will come to see themselves in this way too. One area of evidence arises from the extensive research on the placebo effect, well-illustrated by Davies (2013). If a person believes they are working with someone who is supportive of them, takes them seriously and provides something that will help them to feel better, they feel better. In your teacher role, when you believe a student with a problem is resourceful, successful and hopeful, it is more likely that they will be, strengthening their own solution-focused, growth mindset, which identifies the problem as a challenge to be faced up to and overcome through their own strengths and resources. This has been my experience. I have never had a student who refused to work with me, although some took a little time to engage. And I have never given up and I have not had a student give up on me, despite some severe additional challenges that presented themselves.

The nocebo effect, 'I do harm', is the opposite to placebo, 'I will please'. The nocebo effect is poorly understood and not extensively researched. Someone with a problem experiencing a lack of empathy and understanding, or being disbelieved, may feel hopeless and angry and feel they need to justify their difficulties. The nocebo effect appears to be more powerful than the placebo effect, and for this reason is of great interest to those in the helping professions (Stromberg, 2012). Placebos have a long and respectable history in medicine, and placebo effects play a part in the healing relationship between doctor and patient. The doctor's empathy and positive outlook may be the only tools available in many cases of illness. This could be seen as being far away from the classroom, although the idea that positive beliefs can produce beneficial outcomes and that negative beliefs do the opposite is directly relevant to the issue of behaviour. If you approach a student believing that they are resourceful, successful and hopeful in facing their challenges, better outcomes will be achieved than if the same student were believed to be harmful, unsuccessful and in deficit in some way.

How is this relevant to you as a teacher?

Relationships are vital to good behaviour and as a new teacher you will be hoping to build good working relationships with students, based on trust and respect, characteristics that are related to mindset and beliefs. It is arguably as much the foundation of the teacher's work as it is of the therapist's work (Lambert and Barley, 2001). Personal attributes such as being flexible, honest, respectful, trustworthy, confident, warm, interested and open, and techniques including exploration, reflection, accurate interpretation, and attending to the client's experience contribute positively to the cooperative relationship or alliance (Ackerman & Hilsenroth, 2003).

Connecting management and achievement

School and classroom management are intended to produce a smooth surface for teaching and learning to stand on, to achieve the internationally agreed aim of raising achievement, and yet most programmes that have been trialled to date have resulted in zero gains. One development, formative assessment, can effectively double the speed of student learning. Wiliam (2007) specified the conditions under which it can be claimed to be practiced. These included:

- clarify and sharing learning intentions and criteria for success with students
- engineering effective classroom discussions, questions and learning tasks
- providing feedback that moves learners forward
- activating students as the owners of their own learning
- encouraging students to be instructional resources for one another, using peer assessment and feedback.

Solution-support matches up to this list fairly well, given that Wiliam discussed whole-class assessment and solution-support is primarily for individualized learning. This necessarily limits the opportunity for peer assessment and feedback, but in all other aspects solution-support can be seen to engage the formative assessment cycle. The speed of student learning, as Wiliam put it, in all the cases where I have used solution-support to promote learning, is certainly rapid.

Classroom management and students' behaviour that promotes learning go hand in hand, supported by clear procedures and simple rules to help students remember them. Teaching the class community about procedures and correcting procedural errors is part of the teacher's daily work. Planning your classroom management project can be aided by tools such as logic-modelled planning, which can reduce the clutter and stress you are likely to experience as you set out to teach. But what do you do when thoughtful management does not work? The growth mindset (Dweck, 2006) response is to treat it as a challenge, and an opportunity to make renewed effort. It is time to do something different, and solution-support can provide that difference.

Putting solution-support into action

The solution-focused approach has been growing and expanding in its application since its beginnings in the early 1980s with Steve de Shazer's work as a brief therapist (de Shazer, 1985, 1988). It has been used in schools for more than twenty years by educational psychologists, counsellors and specialist support teachers. A collected work edited by Ajmal and Rees (2001) described a range of applications of solution-focused thinking in schools, including behaviour. The UK government's Department for Education and Skills *Primary Strategy* (2005) included training materials and guidance for using the solution-focused approach to behaviour. The use of the solution-focused approach is developing steadily in schools in the UK and internationally (Mahlberg et al., 2005; Murphy, 2008; Rae and Smith, 2009; Ratner and Yusuf, 2015).

My intention is to support you in your professional development by introducing you to a new approach to behaviour, but I realize that changes in classroom practice are difficult to achieve. Ideas coming from educational research do not tend to penetrate into classrooms, despite a push for evidence-based teaching by Hargreaves in the 1990s (Hargreaves, 1996, 1999) and more recently by Goldacre (2013), the connection between teaching and academic research remains weak. As for research by teachers and schools into their own practice, this has been described as the most difficult field of educational research to conceptualize and in which to see a clear way forward (McIntyre and McIntyre, 1999). This is partly due to the nature of small-scale research *into* practice, which is what teachers do routinely, being quite unlike that of large-scale research *about* practice. Research into practice is highly context-related and does not set out to make the sort of broad, generalizable claims coming out of the large-scale experimental research that Goldacre (2013) was proposing. Research by teachers does make claims, and these are intentionally limited to what Simons et al. (2003) called 'situated generalizations'. Teachers only refine or adopt practices if they connect closely with the situation in which the evidence for improving practice arose. If the situation was sufficiently close, the research findings could be treated as being relevant, at least to the extent of being trialled by a teacher looking for new ideas.

I carried out research into my practice as a behaviour support teacher and took my findings directly into my work into schools, responding to students in need of support with their behaviour and usually with the aim of maintaining their inclusion in school. I invited teachers to join meetings as observers, to take part in solution-support sessions, to take sessions over, to work independently with me supporting them from a distance and ultimately providing supervision for their ongoing solution-focused teaching. With this degree of closeness many teachers, teaching assistants and others have trialled the solution-support method. This experience explains why I have presented evidence as stories from my practice. I hope you can use this evidence to connect with your own immediate experience as a teacher and your general experience having been a student in school.

COMMENT

Practice-based evidence took the solution-focused approach to change-making that Steve de Shazer, Insoo Kim Berg and others developed from the therapy rooms in Milwaukee into the wider world of problem-solving. People came to their clinic looking for change; it happened and the therapists looked at their practice for clues as to what had been useful. Solution-focused theory develops as an explanation of practical solution-focused support. In contrast, evidence-based practice was what Beck (1967) developed in his problem-focused cognitive behavioural therapy (CBT) and Dweck (2006) in her mindset approach to change. Originating in the controlled simplicity of the research laboratory and later applied experimentally to the complexity of the school community may explain why it has been difficult to integrate them into teacher's routine practice in changing behaviour.

The knowledge and skills of staff are the single most important factor in promoting good behaviour. (Steer Report, 2005: 83) I developed my own approach to my work with students who had tested every behaviour management strategy available, and emerged still disrupting and underachieving and generally not doing as they were told. In the process I worked steadily towards simplicity. I freed myself from the demands of formal assessment and diagnosis, remembering that I was working with people, not categories of deficit. Along the way my expertise developed in *not* drawing conclusions, in doing less rather than more in a disciplined way. This approach seemed to liberate students who had got caught up in the cycle of failure and punishment, or those on the narrowing path of withdrawal. I worked with many students who were balancing on the edge of school. I put the approach to the test in apparently hopeless situations, because I felt that I needed to know the limits of its capacity for enabling change to happen. I made it known in my service that I would work with students who were at the point of permanent exclusion, where everyone had tried everything and nothing had worked. I started getting good results. Students stayed in school and found success. Here is a case in point.

Tony's story

Tony was 14 when we met for the first time and had been living with foster carers for many years. The referral from school requesting behaviour support said that he had attacked other students in school, often injuring them. In class he was fine, meeting all his targets and making expected progress. All the strategies written into the school's behaviour policy had been tried but his violent behaviour remained unchanged, nothing worked. The referral stated that Tony had had verbal warnings by his Head of Key Stage, been put in detention and given what they called 'Front of School', a kind of public shaming. He had been excluded for increasingly longer fixed terms and his foster carers had been called into school. They had been told that Tony would be permanently excluded the next time he attacked another student. There were to be no more chances for Tony and there was no alternative open to them in the interests of other students in the school.

Tony had reached the end of the road. I accepted the request to get involved and got to work. I checked out his learning with the school SENCO who had been closely involved in trying to support and guide Tony, but who felt completely stuck. He said Tony had no additional learning needs and was making appropriate progress in class, given that he was frequently being excluded from school or sitting in detention instead of in class.

I met Tony in school, in a tiny office off the busy main special needs room. We shook hands and I asked him where he would like to sit. I told him who I was and why I was there. I said that I got called in to schools particularly to work with students who had got a bit stuck. I asked him if he knew beforehand that this meeting was going to happen, and he said his carers had told him someone called Geoffrey James was coming in to school to meet him, but he did not know why.

Me: Suppose we did some work together Tony, what might we work on that could be useful to you?

Tony: My behaviour?

Me: So if we worked on something to do with your behaviour, that could be useful to you?

Tony: Yeah.

Me: OK. So shall we do that?

Tony: Yeah.

Me: We'll do that then. But first I want to ask you about something completely different. What's your best thing? What do you like doing best?'

Tony: What in school or ...?'

Me: In school, out of school. Anywhere.'

Tony: Oh well, that would be fishing ...'

So we talked about fishing. He knew a lot about it. And then we talked about other things he enjoyed doing. Our first meeting lasted for 40 minutes. The follow-up meetings lasted for between 20 and 30 minutes. We planned to meet five times over a month and then review, to decide whether to end the work or to continue. At the review, Tony said he was not ready to end, so we arranged another set of five weekly meetings. At the next review, again Tony said he would like to continue working together. I asked him what it was about our work that was useful, and he said it gave him a chance to talk about what was going well. I asked him how often we should meet, and he said maybe once a month would be OK.

Over the following terms we met infrequently. In his final year in school we met twice. At our last meeting, in mid-July, he told me he was starting a joinery apprenticeship in the autumn, that had come out of his successful work experience. I asked him again how our work together had been useful to him, and he answered in an interesting way. He said that the chance to talk about what was going well was useful, but the most important thing to him was that he was still the same person I'd met when he was 14. He had grown into a well-built six-footer. He said if he saw his friend being picked on in the street, he'd go to help him, he would get stuck in. He could because he was a good fighter. What had changed was that he knew when to do it and when not to. I said he'd always been good to work with, because of his ability to think about what he did, about being reflective. He thought about it, nodded. I said 'And you're doing it right now!' We shook hands and said a final goodbye.

COMMENT

From that first meeting until the last Tony never had another fight in school, was not temporarily or permanently excluded. What had we been doing since that first conversation about fishing? Solution-focused work, an inquiry into what he was hoping for, what he was good at, and what might change. I had offered no strategies, no rewards, no punishment. He had made the important change in his behaviour that would enable him to stay in school and through it all he did not feel he had been made to change as a person. He felt more able to be the best person he could be, to live up to his potential.

Practice and theory

Practical guides on behaviour management tend to put theoretical issues to one side and emphasize the practicalities of the work. In my own experience of working within a large group of educational psychologists and specialist teachers, we, the teachers, were assumed to be doing entirely practical work, but we were told by our principal psychologist that everything we did had to be based on sound psychological principles.

In the field of behaviour and behaviour management, psychological thinking has come to dominate teacher's practice, whether or not it is clearly understood. Teaching is not psychology and it has a different base. I have found a lack of understanding of what it meant to be teachers 'doing' pedagogy, not psychologists doing experiments. So, in company with other teachers, I made my own way in practical matters. I had real children with real difficulties sitting in front of me, with an immediate need for me to do something useful. To me it was not good enough just to do what had been done before without question, particularly when it was not proving to be effective. Meanwhile a powerful theory, behaviourism, has influenced our practice in a fundamental way, and as reflective practitioners we should interrogate it, to see if it works and if it is what we want.

Is behaviourist reward and punishment the way to address behaviour problems in schools? In Tony's case, the school's behaviour policy supported the assumption that although he did not make the required changes, he was fully able to do so, at any time of his choosing. Each new inconvenience or punishment should have brought about the change; the fact it did not was apparently not good enough reason to do something different in the absence of an alternative. But supposing we assumed that change could happen in a different way, not at the point of punishment, but in the reflective space between something going wrong for Tony and the punishment itself? Some psychologists have offered new ways of looking at behaviour change, and the nature of the change process itself has come under scrutiny.

In 1983 the clinical psychologists Prochaska and DiClemente proposed their transtheoretical model of behaviour change. Existing models focused exclusively on the biological or social dimensions of change, as for example the biological 'stimulus and response' model applied to Tony and his behaviour in school. They drew key aspects from across a range of theories to construct a comprehensive theory of change, some aspects of which were and are controversial, notably the stepped process they proposed (Prochaska and DiClemente, 1983). In 2003, DiClemente published his book *Addiction and Change* which went into detail on the application of the model to research and clinical work. The idea was that long before a person gets involved in the action of actually carrying through a change, they are attempting it. If a person is unsuccessful, it might be due to lack of knowledge, the strength of existing habits or their weak commitment to unclear plans. How does this connect to the work I did with Tony? It was designed to meet his needs, as someone already attempting to change his behaviour. The attempts to change his behaviour that had gone before were based on the assumption that he was resistant, and unmotivated to change. The rather muddled idea that punishment would both overcome his resistance and motivate him, at one and the same time, did not prove to be successful over the many months it was tried. It did not make the difference hoped for, that Tony would stop misbehaving. It certainly appeared that his behaviour was habitual, because it seemed to be so hard to change and as far as was known he did not have any plans that he had spoken of.

Prochaska and DiClemente (1983) worked across the disciplinary boundaries between psychology, biology and sociology to reconceptualize the complexity of human behaviour. They also addressed two aspects of behaviour change ignored in many other theories: that change is a process taking place over time and that the process is non-linear. Behaviour change has its own pace, often happening rapidly and in bursts of activity, periods of inaction and looping back to previous forms of behaviour, as can be seen in the case stories from my practice. The solution-support process matches up to this description of the change process; with rapid change, the finding and strengthening of already successful behaviour, and periods of settlement. I will just note here that the transtheoretical model incorporates self-efficacy theory, developed by Albert Bandura in the late 1970s, and I will develop this connection further in the next chapter.

How is this theoretical thinking relevant to you as a teacher? Our thinking has come to be dominated by non-educationalists, but we can gain professionally and practically from looking over the school wall, in constructing our own educational models of change. It is important to know that you can develop you own educational perspective on behaviour and behaviour change. The transtheoretical model of change was an example of what can be achieved by crossing boundaries. More recently Kinderman (2014) said that we must move away from the disease model, in assuming that biological illness can explain emotional distress. Instead he suggests that we should embrace a psychological and social approach to mental wellbeing that recognizes our essential and shared humanity, but despite these theoretical developments not much has changed in schools. Whether we sign up to the disease model or the psychosocial model, or put them to one side and emphasize a solution-focused pedagogical model of change, it is important that we have a better understanding of the consequences of the choices we make, for ourselves and for the students we teach. We need to get more familiar with the possibilities and limits of various models of change and their roles in education.

COMMENT

You may have come across the term attention deficit hyperactivity disorder (ADHD). While the cause of ADHD is unknown, it is described as a condition of the brain that causes inattention, hyperactivity and impulsivity, most common in school-aged children, affecting an individual throughout life and in many contexts. School students who are diagnosed with ADHD are routinely medicated with powerful stimulant medication, for example Ritalin, classified as a 'class A' drug if not authorized by prescription.

In the UK in 2007, 420,000 prescriptions were written for Ritalin, rising to 657,000 in 2012. An article in the *British Medical Journal*

(Continued)

(Continued)

(Thomas et al., 2013) pointed out that the clinical definition of ADHD has been progressively expanded and ADHD is now the most common behaviour disorder of childhood. In 2009 in the UK 1.5 per cent of children between 6 and 8 were diagnosed with ADHD; in the USA 6.3 per cent of children between 5 and 9 were diagnosed and 11 per cent of 4 to 17 year-olds. Usually there is no distinction made between mild and serious ADHD and it is suggested by some that it should be seen as an ordinary developmental issue rather than a mental disorder in many cases.

What is your response to these statistics, as a teacher? How should you respond to inattentive or overactive students in your class? Thomas et al. (2013) point out that in the UK, the National Institute for Health and Care Excellence (NICE) guidelines recommend a stepped approach and that psychological treatment is given priority over drug treatment, but this still adopts the medical definition with the need for treatment. Maybe an early step could be a pedagogical one, like using solution-support as a teaching approach to the behavioural issues of inattention or overactivity? I have found it useful in my own work.

Conclusion

Sometimes students break rules. When that happens something has to be done because a community needs commonly-observed rules to map out the boundaries of behaviour. Across a school community, most students follow most of the rules most of the time, otherwise the place would be in chaos. If you look carefully you can see students following rules in a good enough way, as they move from place to place and from one activity to another during the school day. If they break a rule it is usually easy to get them back with a smile and a word. Some students intentionally cross a boundary to see if it is real, and when it is pointed out to them they comply readily enough. It is an important part of a student's learning to know that some rules are negotiable while others are not. For example, many schools have rules about what students should wear, and there may be a degree of flexibility, with senior students allowed to make some choices for themselves, or they may be strictly defined and enforced. Other rules, like the carrying of any form of knife into school, are non-negotiable, and this reflects life outside the school gates.

As a beginning teacher you can feel confident that what you know already you can use effectively with most of the students you will work with. If you need more guidance at this stage, a great deal has already been written about rules and reminders by authors such as Bill Rogers and Sue Cowley, so I am not going to add to it here. This book is about something different. A few students do not seem to know the rules, or they have other things in their lives that soak up their attention. This is where school behaviour policies come in, detailing the support and graded punishments intended to shape the offender's behaviour back to compliance. If the strategies work, students remain safely in school with all the opportunities available to them there. There is plenty of advice from behaviour experts about what to do with these students to get them to comply.

Some students, like Tony, exhaust all the strategies written in the school behaviour policy and some receive the final punishment of permanent exclusion from their own school community. A very small number of students in any school seem to resist all attempts to help them or to force them to comply. When strategies do not work, students' lives can be severely affected. Some students are much more likely to become permanently excluded from school than their peers, on the grounds of their disruptive and unacceptable behaviour. Many of these are students with disabilities and additional educational needs, and those who are living in local authority homes or in foster care, like Tony.

For teachers, it becomes progressively more difficult for us to understand what our role should be in trying to ensure the inclusion of these students. Some students do have disorders and disabilities, and the sooner their medical needs are identified and appropriate support and treatment put in place the better. We can play a part in that by using the solution-focused approach initially, and when we review progress if the work has not proved useful, make a referral outwards to the additional support systems in school. But for students who are in the process of making personal sense of the world and making mistakes along the way, as teachers we can make a real, useful and positive difference and solution-support offers an accessible and useful approach to take.

References

Ackerman, S. and Hilsenroth, M. (2003) 'A review of therapist characteristics and techniques positively impacting the therapeutic alliance', *Clinical Psychology Review*, 23: 1–33.

Ajmal, Y., Rees, I. (2001) *Solutions in Schools: Creative Applications of Solution Focused Brief Thinking with Young People and Adults*. London: BT Press.

Beck, A. T. (1967) *Depression – Clinical Experimental and Theoretical Aspects*. New York: Harper and Row.

Davies J. (2013) *Cracked: Why Psychiatry is Doing More Harm Than Good*. London: Icon Books.

de Shazar, S. (1985) *Keys to Solutions in Brief Therapy*. New York: Norton.

de Shazar, S. (1988) *Clues: Investigating Solutions in Brief Therapy*. New York: Norton.

Department for Education and Skills (DfES) (2005) 'Primary strategy'. Available at: http://webarchive.nationalarchives.gov.uk/20130401151715/www.education.gov.uk/publications/eOrderingDownload/DFES0110200MIG2122.pdf (accessed 1 May 2015).

DiClemente, C. C. (2003) *Addiction and Change: How Addictions Develop and Addicted People Recover*. New York: Guilford Press.

Dweck, C. S. (2006) *Mindset: The New Psychology of Success*. New York: Random House.

Freiberg, H. J. (2002) 'Redesigning professional development', *Essential Skills for New Teachers*, 59 (6): 56–60.

Funnell, S. and Rogers, P. (2011) *Purposeful Program Theory: Effective Use of Theories of Change and Logic Models*. San Francisco, CA: Wiley.

Goldacre, B. (2013) 'Teachers! What would evidence based practice look like?' Available at: www.badscience.net/2013/03/heres-my-paper-on-evidence-and-teaching-for-the-education-minister/#more-2849 (accessed 1 May 2015).

Hargreaves, D. (1996) 'Teaching as a research-based profession: Possibilities and prospects'. Teacher Training Agency Annual Lecture 1996, London.

Hargreaves, D. (1999) 'Revitalizing educational research: Lessons from the past and proposals for the future', *Cambridge Journal of Education*, 29: 239–49.

Kinderman, P. (2014) *A Prescription for Psychiatry: Why We Need a Whole New Approach to Mental Health and Wellbeing*. London: Palgrave Macmillan.

Lambert, M. J. and Barley, D. E. (2001) 'Research summary on the therapeutic relationship and psychotherapy outcome', *Psychotherapy: Theory, Research, Practice, Training*, 38 (4): 357.

Mahlberg, K., Sjoblom, M. and McKergow, M. (2005) 'Solution Focused Education'. Available at: http://sfwork.com/pdf/sfeducation.pdf (accessed March 2015).

McIntyre, D. and McIntyre, A. (1999) *Capacity for Research into Teaching and Learning: Report to the Programme*. Swindon: ESRC Teaching and Learning Research Programme.

Murphy, J. J. (2008) 'Solution-focused counseling in schools'. Based on a program presented at the ACA Annual Conference & Exhibition, Honululu, HI. Available at: http://counselingoutfitters.com/vistas/vistas08/Murphy.htm (accessed 3 November 2015).

Prochaska, J. and DiClemente, C. (1983) 'Stages and processes of self-change in smoking: Toward an integrative model of change', *Journal of Consulting and Clinical Psychology*, 5: 390–95.

Rae, T. and Smith, E. (2009) *Teaching Tools: A Solution Focused Approach for Secondary Staff and Students*. London: Optimus Education.

Ratner, H. and Yusuf, D. (2015) *Brief Coaching with Children and Young People: A Solution Focused Approach*. London: Routledge.

Simons, H., Kushner, S., Jones, K. and James, D. (2003) 'From evidence-based practice to practice-based evidence: The idea of situated generalization', *Research Papers in Education*, 18 (4): 347–64.

Steer Report, The (2005) *Learning Behaviour: The Report of the Practitioners' Group on School Behaviour and Discipline*. London: Department for Education and Skills.

Stromberg, J. (2012) 'What is the Nosebo effect?' Available at: www.smithsonianmag.com/science-nature/what-is-the-nocebo-effect-5451823/#KOfiLE4jEiQEhZMq.99 (accessed March 2015).

Thomas, R. Mitchell, G. K. Batstra, L. (2013) Attention deficit/hyperactivity disorder: are we helping or harming? *British Medical Journal* 347:f6172-2.

Thoreau, H. D. (1995 [1854]) *Walden: Or, Life in the Woods* (Dover Thrift Editions). USA: Dover Publications Inc.

Wiliam, D. (2007) 'Changing classroom practice', *Educational Leadership*, 65 (4): 36–42.

4

DEVELOPING CONFIDENCE IN PRACTICE

This chapter will give you the opportunity to:

- think about what can affect your confidence as a teacher

- explore your level of confidence about the issue of behaviour

- envisage where you hope to be in terms of your confidence in a year's time, and the first steps you will take to get there

- engage in the process of professional development which will lead to your confident success in class over time

Newly qualified teachers consistently identify behaviour management as an area of practice where they need more support (Powell and Tod, 2004). In 2008, the Organization for Economic Co-operation and Development (OECD) reported that one-third of new teachers said they needed training and support concerning student discipline and behaviour problems, and did not feel effective in these areas.

As you set out on your teaching career, it is important that you feel confident, purposeful and effectual, in the interests of the students and yourself. Here we are interested in being confident about behaviour in class. Approaching the development of your practice by recognizing what is going well, and where something could usefully be changed, has the power to strengthen your successful practice and enjoyment of teaching and your feelings of confidence.

In many areas of activity – including education, industry, commerce, sport, psychotherapy and medicine – a new approach to personal and professional growth and development is rapidly gaining ground. It focuses on building successes, strengths and resources, and it represents a shift away from the traditional trial and error, with a focus on failures. You might see it referred to as the strengths approach, the solution-focused approach, or solution-focused coaching. In relation to the behaviour of students in school, I call this approach solution-support.

EXERCISE

Think about a time when you used your existing strengths-based skills, where you focused on successes and hopes for the future, with someone who came to you for asking for support. It might have been over a very small problem, and it might have seemed insignificant at the time.

- What kind of feedback did you give them?

- What were your beliefs and values that underpinned the supportive work you did at the time?

The power of feedback

Hattie (1992) identified feedback from the teacher to the student as the most powerful factor in improving achievement. Later he wrote that he had made a mistake in defining feedback as something teachers provided *to* students. It must include feedback *from* students on their state of engagement, their knowledge and understanding. When this two-way communication happens, teaching and learning is improved (Hattie, 2009: 173).

Feedback and its powerful effect on learning are at the heart of solution-support, positioning the student as an active agent in his or her own learning and growth, rather than as a passive recipient of information or advice. It provides the student with a degree of control, and engages them as responsible change-makers. Students' motivation to learn and change is affected by the degree to which they feel in control of their learning experience (Hattie, 2009: 47–49) and their internal, intrinsic motivation is progressively weakened as increasing external control is exercised by their teacher.

REFLECTION

- From what you know already, what effect can external discipline have on the self-motivation of a student who is trying to change their behaviour?

Developing a confident attitude towards student behaviour is an important aspect of your professional development at this stage of your career. It is aided by being in control of your own learning experience, as a student of teaching.

This strengthens your internal motivation. Experiencing the process of your own growth in confidence will give you a better understanding of the parallel process your students undertake as they grow and develop.

Evidence-informed professional development

Wiliam (2012) took a close look at the research evidence relating to teacher development. He suggested that it is most effective when two developmental questions are addressed in order:

1. Content: What is the task?
2. Process: How can I do it?

A task you may face as a beginning teacher is to strengthen your confidence with regard to behaviour in class, moving to a situation where it does not interfere with the overall focus of your teaching. A newly qualified teacher, Ben, was struggling with behaviour in his classroom, and losing confidence in himself – and I was asked to help if I could. This is another example of solution-support in action. As the story unfolds, make notes on what catches your interest and what you feel curious about, and how your own experience compares to Ben's. Also make a note of your impression of the purpose of each part of the conversation. The pattern of the inquiry in solution-support is always the same, so as you read this story, you are getting another real insight into how it works in practice, as a useful model for your own work.

EXERCISE

Draw two scales in your notebook. Where would you put yourself on the first scale, for how things are now?

1 10

Behaviour is a worry for me   Behaviour is no worry for me

Where do you hope you might be on this scale, one term from now?

1 10

Worry   No worry

If you are somewhere on the scale other than 10, what is one small thing that you might do differently, to get you nearer to 10?

Case story: Constructing confidence

I was the behaviour support teacher for a secondary school, for half a day per week over several years. Briefing the Deputy Headteacher with responsibility for behaviour on my current work in the school one day, he asked me:

DH: Does solution-support work as well with adults as it does with children?

Me: Yes, it does.

DH: We've got a newly qualified teacher (NQT) who's really struggling with behaviour. He says he's thinking of giving up teaching. We're supporting him as much as we can, but things aren't improving. I wonder if you could work with him?'

The Deputy Head asked me to do an observation with a class that Ben, the NQT, was finding difficult to manage. He had arranged cover so that Ben and I could meet in the period following the observation. I said that I had reservations about the usefulness of observation in general, but I would do a solution-focused observation as it could be useful to Ben. I said I would ask Ben first and if he agreed, then I would go into a class with him and talk to him afterwards, as suggested.

A few days later, I met Ben in the staffroom at morning break time. He said the Deputy Head had outlined my approach, and that he suggested I would observe him teaching the chosen class, if he thought it would be useful. He said he was disappointed about how things were going, that he came into teaching because he wanted to pass on his love of history, but now he felt like giving up.

Ben had a strong regional accent. He said he thought that must be the main problem, that his students could not understand him. He had even tried to find a voice coach to help him get rid of his accent, but without success. I said I noticed his commitment and his hopefulness, still trying his best despite things being tough in class.

I asked him to tell me about a time when behaviour did not get in the way of teaching and things went well, and he soon found an exception to the difficulties that were dragging him down. I asked him to tell me what had gone well, what was already working. Then I asked him:

Me: What is it about you, that contributed to success in that class?

I was curious about his strengths and resources and wanted to hear his description of them. He suggested a number of them, and we talked about them for a few minutes.

Me: How about another time when things went well?

Me: And another time

He recalled a number of successes with different classes.

Me: If you did want me to come into your class, I'd be looking out for what's working and making a few notes. We could talk immediately afterwards. Shall we do that?

Ben: Ay.

I arranged to come in to his classroom the following week. As I waited in the corridor for the lesson to start, the students clattered in and sat down. There was plenty of talking, calling across the room, looking out of the windows. Ben began writing the lesson objectives on the whiteboard, but broke off to move around the room while the students settled down. I sat at the back of the room. He introduced me briefly as a teacher observing the lesson, and went to write the remaining lesson objectives on the white board. The students started chatting and he raised his voice to quieten them, to get started with the lesson.

A few minutes before the bell, he reviewed the learning objectives with the class and the students clattered out again.

We sat down to talk about what happened.

Ben: It wasn't good was it? They came in OK, but they started chatting again. Then it's hard to be heard.

Me: Mmmm. When we planned this session, I said I was going to be looking out for what went well. What did you notice that was 'good enough' at the start?

He took a while to think about this.

Ben: Well, when the students came in they did get settled, and only started chatting whilst I was writing on the board. So getting settled the first time was OK.

Me: I made a note of that myself. So what is it about you as a teacher that made that go well?

Ben: Well, I know to walk around the room when students come in, to help them settle down. I always do that.

> *Me*:   So something about you walking around the room, being avail-
> able to students at the start, as they settle down, and doing that
> as a routine? Is that right?
>
> *Ben*:   Yes.

We talked in detail about what went well, the strengths and resources he
brought to his teaching. I didn't give him any advice, my notes were there to
help me recall the story, not for analysis. My role was to guide the inquiry.
This part of our conversation lasted for 15 minutes.

I asked him to scale his confidence in his teaching, where 10 was 'good
enough to keep going' and one was 'giving up'. He put himself at six, where
if he was actually just about to give up, he might have placed himself nearer
to one. I asked him what was telling him that he was already at six, and he
came up with several things that were going well enough.

In solution-focused terminology, this is called pre-sessional change. Ben
was already making changes towards his best hope, even before we met for
the observation and feedback session. It is a phenomenon commonly seen
in support work; since Ben wanted to make changes, why not get started
right away, after we had met to arrange our work together?

> *Me*:   Do you hope you'll stay at six or might there be a change?'

He said he hoped they might change and I asked him where he might be in
a month's time. He said 'Eight'.

> *Me*:   What's the smallest thing that you might do differently in your
> next class, to move you towards eight?'
>
> *Ben*:   Write the learning objectives up before the students come in.

When our time was nearly up, I said there were two things Ben needed to
do, a compliment and a task, with the compliment first. I asked him to
compliment himself. He thought about it for a minute or two.

> *Ben*:   That even though things have been bad, I haven't given up.
>
> *Me*:   So it's something about you, as a person who hasn't given up yet,
> you keep trying to make it work?
>
> *Ben*:   Yes.
>
> *Me*:   My compliment to you is about you inviting me into a difficult
> situation with your class, to do this work. It's about you being
> confident enough to do that. Is that true about you?

Ben: Yeah, I guess so.

Me: The last thing is to offer you a task; it's to notice things going well. Notice what's going well for you and where you are on your scale. For example, where might you put yourself right now?

Ben: Well, it's up a bit, maybe near seven?

Me: Up a bit. Well, thanks very much Ben. Good luck with your teaching.

As we were finishing, I mentioned that if he needed to meet again, he could ask the Deputy Head to contact me. I didn't hear anything.

Six months later on a regular visit, I saw him in the crowded staffroom and we nodded and smiled across the room. The Deputy Head was there and I asked him if things were going well enough. He said Ben had started the new school year positively.

EXERCISE

Think about a time when there might have been a behaviour problem in a class you were teaching, you took the opportunity to do something creative and things went well as a result. Make a note of it, and then think about four other occasions when you did something creative, and things went well as a result. Make a note of them.

Draw a scale in your notebook. Where would you put yourself on the scale, for how things are right now?

1 10

Behaviour worries me   Behaviour doesn't worry me

At a good time, maybe in a month, go back to the worry/no worry scale to see where you are, what is working and what you might change a bit.

Why take the solution-focused approach to a problem?

The work Ben and I did together focused on what was working. When a problem comes up, the usual thing is to make the problem itself the centre of attention and look for what is not working. If Ben had gone to a problem-focused expert for help, he might have been asked a series of questions like these:

'What's wrong?'

'When did the problem start?'

'How often does it happen?'

'How does it make you feel?'

'What have you tried so far to overcome it?'

The expert asks for detailed information on the problem, in order to identify what caused it. They check out any strategies that have been tried, and failed. Using their expert knowledge they suggest strategies for you to try out, to eliminate the problem. The accuracy of their informed guess is confirmed or disproved by the results. If the problem goes away, all is well. If it is still there, they suggest an alternative strategy to try out.

My approach with Ben was solution-focused, not problem-focused: we looked for signs of success, for what was already working, moving towards the solution of his problem in the future.

In my first conversation with Ben, before we had got as far as the classroom, he started by telling me about the problem, what caused it and his strategy to solve it. He naturally assumed we would look at the problems, and he had almost decided the problem was too big and it would defeat him. He was getting close to losing his belief in his ability to succeed, as not being self-effectual.

According to Bandura (1994) people with low perceived self-efficacy show a number of general characteristics:

- They avoid difficult tasks which they interpret as personal threats.
- They have low aspirations and a weak commitment to their chosen goals.
- When faced with difficult tasks, they focus on their personal deficiencies and on the obstacles they will meet and that might defeat them.
- They imagine all kinds of things going wrong, rather than concentrating on the process of how to perform successfully.
- They make less effort in trying to succeed, and give up quickly in the face of difficulties.
- They are slow to recover their sense of self-efficacy following a failure or a setback.
- A relatively small failure will cause them to lose faith in their capability because they attribute poor performance to their own personal deficiency.
- They are likely to experience stress and depression.

REFLECTION

- How does Ben map against this list, before and after the work we did together?
- How can you account for the rapid change?

I had been told by Ben's manager and by Ben himself that he might give up, that he felt he was failing. He had identified something very personal, his natural speaking voice, as a possible cause of his failure. But it turned out that his potential was still there, and by focusing in detail on what was working, he could switch his attention away from failure and towards success, to think differently about his relationship to the problem. His mind map, the physical equivalent in the body of the virtual object – the mindset of failure – weakened, and his strength and success mind map recovered and became more active.

When you have a problem, if you think about it and talk about, it seems to grow and get stronger. Even if it is only an anticipated worry, which might never happen, you can think and talk it into existence and can grow it into a major concern. The more you think about it, the stronger it gets, the related mind map becomes more active.

REFLECTION

Most of the things we worry about never happen. Think about your first experiences in the classroom: what were you worried about the night before, when you thought about your Monday morning start, and as you travelled to work, and as you stepped through the classroom door? If something did catch you out as you made a start with your first class of the week, it is likely that it was something unexpected. As a teacher there are many things you have to carry in your mind, many that go well and some that could go wrong. You try to cover them all in your planning. If you focus on problems and failures it is more likely that you will see problems as brick walls, rather than challenges to be overcome by steady effort and focus. Instead of this, you could think about what has gone well, something you did that was quite difficult and led to a good result through your own efforts and skill, and that made a difference to your whole week. You will naturally settle on something worthwhile, because the successes you achieved with very little effort are insignificant. If you think about doing more of it in the week ahead, noticing the result and noting it in your journal, imagined worries will dissipate. As you step into your classroom, you will have your project in mind and be curious about how it goes. Who knows, you might even involve your students in the doing of it. If you can find 20 minutes on a Sunday, try it out.

Ben had been selectively paying attention to what was going wrong, and began to see himself as an incompetent person. He repeated mistakes, until he came to the conclusion that he did not have what it takes to be a teacher. When he refocused on his successes, he recovered his underlying sense of self-efficacy, which is evident when you check what you now know about Ben against Bandura's (1994) list above.

I have worked with people of all ages, in many different situations, who have felt stuck in apparently hopeless situations, becoming increasingly unsure about themselves, and in their ability to make changes and to succeed. In the early days of my job as a support teacher, I knew only how to use the problem-focused approach to problem solving. I was positioned as the expert in behaviour, collecting the information, analysing the problem, identifying its cause and suggesting the remedy. Too often I became stuck too, and could not figure out what to do. Sometimes I did not make things any better for the students I was trying to help, when the complexity of their problem exceeded my expertise. It just was not good enough as professional work, and it motivated me to keep looking for a way of working which was reliably effective, fair and ethical – the work of a teacher.

Focusing on solutions

I found what I was looking for in the solution-focused approach to problem solving: solution-support. It was the approach I took with the history teacher, Ben, and his problems. By paying full attention to his existing resourcefulness and competence, and to the successes produced through the action of his strengths, solution-support systematically blocks the problem mind map and its associated experiences of failure and prevents it from dominating the conversation.

Identifying previously unnoticed or unemphasized flashes of success as evidence of competence altered Ben's view of himself, away from mostly-failing towards sometimes-succeeding as a teacher. Searching for detail about these flashes results in Ben rebuilding his story of Ben-the-competent-teacher. As he reflects on his strengths and resources that bring about these flashes of success, he increasingly sees himself as competent, and he becomes more confident. This is a feedback loop, where noticing success builds success. By blocking the failure mind map, Ben's success mind map becomes more available. On the principle of 'use it or lose it', it becomes stronger the more it is exercised, by exploring the flashes of success in conversation. Conversely, the failure mind map becomes weakened. In Ben's case this process was very quick, and I have seen this rapid jump from failure to success happen repeatedly in the years I have been doing this work.

At first it seemed an unlikely outcome of a brief conversation, but later I came to rely on it happening, and I could confidently relax in addressing what had previously seemed like stuck problems.

Bandura (1994) gave us an image of a person with a high level of perceived self-efficacy, as someone who chooses to take on tasks that will stretch them, and who sees the demand inherent in the task as an interesting challenge. They do not easily give up and when things get tough they respond by making more effort, confident in their ability to retain their sense of control. If they do have a failure they see it as temporary, and take it as a useful nudge towards getting more information or developing a skill in preparation for the next time. Someone with this outlook usually succeeds in what they set out to do, and if they do not succeed they are resilient to setbacks and prepared to accept a new challenge.

Recalling Ben's experience, he demonstrated the complexity of his thinking in his situation by showing some developing signs of low perceived self-efficacy in considering giving up, and of high perceived self-efficacy in keeping going in the face of a tough challenge. He was prepared to make another effort, after a considerable period of struggle, without achieving success. While he had spoken about giving up, in practice he showed resilience in re-entering the classroom every day, and literally bounced back after our short piece of work together. While his performance in class did not reliably demonstrate it, his high self-efficacy mind map was well-developed, and the focus on strengths and successes reactivated it. From my long experience of solutions-focused working, in asking him to focus on success both before, during and after our meeting, I knew that there was a good chance of the success mind map strengthening and the blocked problem mind map weakening.

As a beginning teacher you will find some aspects of the work challenging, and behaviour is known to trouble many new teachers, as it did Ben. With a strong sense of perceived self-efficacy, you will be better at choosing appropriate challenges to address and be more resilient as you go about the process of change. To recap, characteristics of a person with a strong sense of efficacy are:

- They set themselves significant goals and approach difficult tasks as challenges rather than as threats to be avoided.
- If they are stretched in doing the task, they increase and sustain their efforts.
- If they fail they quickly recover their sense of efficacy and look to increase their skills and knowledge, to make a new attempt if the goal is still significant.

(Bandura, 1994)

What factors affect self-efficacy and where does solution-support fit into the picture? Solution-support focuses on success, on the solution to a problem already happening, on resourcefulness and strengths. When a person recognizes their own success, their own expertise in relation to the challenges they encounter, it has the effect of raising their perceived self-efficacy, which can improve their own performance. There are a number of factors affecting a person's sense of self-efficacy, the most important being this perception of expertise, what Bandura (1994) termed the experience of being expert, or 'mastery', and proposed other factors. I will say more about the experience of being expert after briefly looking at modelling, social persuasion and physiology as contributory factors.

Modelling

When we see someone succeeding with a task, our own perceived self-efficacy increases, and when we see someone failing, it decreases. It is a gentle influence, useful for people who tend not to notice their own competence, as is the case when a student gets into a cycle of failure in class. The effect is enhanced when the person modelling success is perceived as being similar to us in some way. There are ways in which students could see you as being similar to themselves in some ways, and a model of competence and self-efficacy.

REFLECTION

- Are you the teacher who always knows the answer, or are you sometimes as puzzled as your students, and do you share that with them?

- Do you talk about being unsure and go to find out together?

- Do you talk about the idea that some learning might be quite hard work, and explain why you still have to do it?

- Do you take a solution-focused approach to problems that come up, working as a team of detectives investigating success?

- Do you get a chance to share classrooms with other teachers, and talk about successes and hoped-for changes afterwards?

Social persuasion

Being encouraged or discouraged by other people impacts on a person's perceived self-efficacy. Discouragement has a stronger effect in lowering someone's self-efficacy than encouragement has in raising it. If a student is punished in the hope of discouraging them from breaking a rule, it is important to reflect on the intended outcome.

REFLECTION

If you intend the student to feel bad about their action, with justice being seen to be done, is the intended gain sufficient to outweigh their likely loss of self-efficacy, when you remember the effects of low-self efficacy on achievement? Of course, this is estimated against risk and safety to the student and others.

- What is the effect of punishing a student on your own perceived self-efficacy as a teacher?

- What could you do instead, knowing what you do about self-efficacy, to bring about learning and change?

Physiology

The physiological factor is something you might experience in your early days of teaching. It is the physical feelings you experience when you realize that this is it, the students are all looking to you, all your pre-preparation is done, and you are on the stage with the spotlight on you. If I go back to my own experience, I recall being in a room as a new teacher where the students were effectively beyond my control, too loud, moving about, chatting and calling to each other. The lesson had been set out properly, objectives in place, materials ready, all the planning done. I felt angry and upset. I turned to the board on the pretence of writing something, took some deep breaths, thought through the immediate options and about how I could survive. I turned back to the class and sat down, put my marker pen down, put my hands in my lap, and said nothing. Within a few minutes the room was quieter. One of the students asked me if I was going to start teaching her some science. I agreed to, but only for her and because she was prepared to work. We made a start, others joined in, crowded around my table. We spent the remainder of the lesson like that, working at one table. These students were in this school because they had emotional and behavioural difficulties, and it was my job to lead us calmly away from the immediate problem. I do not know how I came to do what I did, but thinking turned out to be a better option than acting at that time. It was an idea I developed in my research writing later, that sometimes doing nothing is the best doing (James, 2007). If you become aware of your physiological reaction to a stressful situation, it is possible to see the experience as a natural one, and breathe your way through it. Maybe you can even smile in realization of your own resourceful calmness – your perceived self-efficacy will rise and this will be evident to students as you model success with a difficult task.

REFLECTION

What works best for you, if and when you experience these natural sensations?
Think back to a time when you were in a situation where you could have been overwhelmed, but instead you took a step back, regained your calmness and carried on. Then do more of what works.

Decision making

There is a great deal of interest in the process of decision making, its control and how it affects people's actions. Research over a variety of fields, including business, organizational behaviour, academic psychology, education sport, music and other professional and creative work, demonstrates that knowing about how you make decisions makes a real difference to the decisions you make. Daniel Kahneman produced a very readable account in his book *Thinking Fast and Slow* (2011). Decision making is of direct relevance to you as a beginning teacher, as you think about behaviour and your response to it, and informs the title for the book.

In essence, there are two interacting, decision-making processes. One is automatic, fast, effortless, and goes into action as a direct response to what is happening around you. It does not discriminate between options, and it may deliver the easiest rather than the best decision, making errors of recency, availability or habit. The other process is regulated, it is slower and requires more effort. As Kahneman (2011) puts it, it is easily tired, and tends to give way to the effortless automatic process. This slower process is the one that holds steadily to the goal that the decision-making process is to deliver or abandon. This controlled process organizes and monitors things such as the appropriateness of the goal, what information is relevant and what should be ignored, and it blocks irrelevant strategies and habits.

Behaviour is guided usually by the automatic process, especially when the controlled process is exhausted by too many demands being made on it. If a person is an expert in an area of practice, the two processes work together to produce fast, controlled and accurate decisions. If you observe an experienced and expert teacher in their well-managed classroom, their fluent practice may seem to be automatic and effortless. However, it takes time and effort to develop expertise. Until you have it, being a new teacher relying on the automatic, impulsive process and on possibly inappropriate and ineffectual habits can lead to poor decision making. So the question is, how can you promote the controlled process over the automatic process? If it is easily tired and subject to overload, then focusing your activity on what is important and achievable in the short- to medium-term, selecting your goals in a systematic way and paying attention to possible biases and habits will reduce the load. Does this sound like a role for solution-focused thinking and logic-modelled project planning? If so, go to Chapter 10.

The experience of being expert, the idea of flow and reflecting on your own self-efficacy

Bandura (1994) proposed that the experience of being expert is the most significant factor in raising a person's perceived self-efficacy. Closely related to this is the work of Mihály Csíkszentmihályi, a positive psychologist who published *Flow: The Psychology of Optimal Experience* in 1990. When you are in flow you are experiencing being expert. Flow happens when a challenging task is matched by, or slightly exceeds, well-developed skills. Given a task of that kind, if you know where you are going, what to do and how to do it, you get feedback and you have a chance to concentrate and work on the project in a creative way, you might enjoy making the effort and experience flow (Schaffer, 2013). Going beyond our specific focus here on behaviour, this has interesting implications for how you design your overall teaching, as a process promoting engagement, creativity and feedback from multiple sources.

REFLECTION

- Do you believe that the process of teaching is as important as the product?

- How would you argue for your position with someone who had the opposite belief?

As a pedagogical model, flow theory has elements of behaviourism because the instructor sets the level of learning-task difficulty, and provides positive reinforcement through feedback; however, this would only be true when the teacher is acting as an instructor uses the behaviourist instruction model. Solution-support is inquiry not instruction, and is constructivist rather than behaviourist. In this case the student selects their own internally consistent goals, given that the overall project has been agreed and the choice is usually constrained in schools, and sets achievable task parameters. As for feedback, if you take the biological view, it happens internally, in addition to feedback given by the teacher. In the case stories I have included in this book, the person making the change gets immediate feedback when he or she looks out for success and finds it, and when they relate their achievement to their own success scale. The teacher using solution-support is a facilitator of inquiry, not an instructional technician.

The term 'flow' has a sense of continuation, for minutes or even hours, but flow can happen over a long time or in an instant, as 'flash-flow'. In my own case, I experience flash-flow as I am in the process of doing solution-focused work. In the process I monitor myself to stay in the moment, to ensure that I pay full attention. I could ask a number of different questions in response to a previous answer. I relax and wait for the question to form itself. When a student recalls a success, they are in the process of telling themself what is already working, what they can do next to make the difference they are hoping for. Many times, in those moments of asking the right question and hearing the powerful answer, I have felt a shiver, a tingle, a flash of flow. Particularly when I asked for my partner in the work to tell me about an exception, when a problem could have occurred but did not, and after a little thought it emerged, I would then experience a surge of happiness and confidence. I knew at this point that we would make progress, and the path ahead was clear.

This degree of subjectivity in my writing at this point might seem surprising, when we are looking at the serious subject of behaviour and at evidence to support the use of a student-centred approach to changing behaviour. But the subjective experience of the researcher engaged in research, in this case myself immersed in an inquiry, has gained significant respectability, for two reasons. The first is that before the idea of reflexivity grew in the 1980s in sociological and psychological research, it was accepted that a researcher could observe other people, as if they (the researcher) could see and perceive without being influenced by their own experience, that they could objectively view other people. From the traditional perspective, subjectivity could only cause damage to the research process, but following the reflexive turn, it became valued as another source of evidence. The second reason is that the traditional approach to this type of research demanded a clear distinction between the researcher and the researched. If the researcher lost objectivity, the research would be tainted. This meant that the emotional dimension and the information related to it was not only neglected but actively avoided (Davies and Spencer, 2010).

The experience of flow, such as that occurring in the course of doing solution-focused work, promotes happiness (Lyubomirsky, 2007). That has been my experience and many other people who I have trained to use the solution-focused approach have reported it. Because of the traditional views of research evidence being so pervasive, the idea that flow and happiness can be outcomes of the sometimes difficult and emotionally demanding work of supporting children and young people in distress is not well developed. But it is worth bearing in mind.

REFLECTION

- Think of a time when you were in flow. How does it match up to the ideas of challenge, skill, feedback and success? What does it tell you about challenge and happiness?

Case story: All in a flash

I am working with 9-year-old Nick, at a distance, using online conferencing. He was diagnosed with Asperger syndrome when he was five, and we worked together then, when he was experiencing great difficulty in his infant school. He is making a success of primary school and overcoming some difficulties too, in social times in school. We're having a 20-minute review meeting and I'm asking him to scale 'school' on a 1–10 scale, where 10 is 'Things going really well' and 1 is the opposite. He's telling me about what he's noticed that tells him things are going well.

He tells me he is learning new things, he is being patient, getting good at telling the time, playing with his friend.

Nick: It could be 9 or 10 Geoffrey, and it's ... 8'.

Before I can comment he adds:

Nick: What would you say Geoffrey, about what I'm doing right now? Would you put me at 10 or 9 or ...? What would you say Geoffrey?

He does this in our conversations: he picks up the language I'm using to frame my questions and asks me a direct question like this.

Me: Hmm ..... What would I say? I'd put you at 10.

Suddenly, he sits up straight and then sits forward, looking directly at me, with his eyes and mouth wide open. He looks amazed. He looks at me like this for a few moments, very close to his screen. Moving his hands and arms, he raises his eyebrows and says excitedly:

Nick: Now I'll put myself at 9 Geoffrey ... I'll put myself at 9 on the scale Geoffrey!

I see this as a Nick's flash-flow. Success strengthens self-efficacy.

Understanding being expert

Anders Ericsson, carrying out research on expertise, said that it takes 10,000 hours of practice in order to achieve expert performance in any field. But that depends on what it is you are practicing (Goleman, 2013).

Goleman (2013) used the metaphor of a golfer to illustrate this, saying that if the golfer made some basic mistakes at the start, and practiced making the same error over 10,000 hours, he would not be a better golfer, just an older one. It is the continuous adjustment of performance towards a hoped-for goal that makes for expert performance. The built-in cycle of action, feedback and adjusted action, though the agency of the person hoping for change, distinguishes solution-support from problem-focused advice and guidance.

Taking Ben's experience as an example, he had flashes of success in the history lesson he prepared and taught, which I witnessed. Broadly, in all of his lessons, even those which superficially looked like failures, there would have been signs of success but they might have passed unnoticed. When we talked after the lesson he said that he noticed his peak performances as the momentary sensations of flash-flow. If I had been responsible for Ben's development as an external expert, I would have had to repeatedly observe his teaching, suggest strategies to improve it and check to see if he had carried them out and whether or not they were successful. By engaging him as the agent of change, modelling solution-support and asking him to continue noticing what was working and what might change, he was on the path of continuous reflection, adjustment and improvement, with successes interpreted as flow in the specific areas of practice that were significant to him.

REFLECTION

You will experience flash-flow as you are teaching. You may or may not notice it at the time, when your own high level of skill matches the challenges you meet, as it takes practice to stay reflectively in the moment and do demanding work at the same time. But you can spot those nuggets of teaching gold by regularly reflecting on your practice, at the time or later on. What is important here is systematically paying attention to your successes, no matter how small or short-lived, to notice what is already working. You will be strengthening your skills, improving your performance from the start and gradually assembling your full repertoire. Paying attention to your successes makes it more likely that you will have more successes to notice. If you think you're doing better you probably will be. If you model the habit of searching systematically for success, your students will perceive a greater sense of their self-efficacy too.

While this chapter is about you and your own confidence as a teacher, you will see in this book that experiencing and noticing flash-flow has the same effect on students as it has on you.

Case story: The flash of artistry

May was 15 and in a lot of trouble in school, not working, uncooperative and moody, according to school reports. At the start of our work together, she had difficulty in remembering things she was good at, while her failures came readily to mind. I'd been told by a teacher that she was a top player in the local women's football league, but she didn't mention it. She was serious about our work and did not smile much.

May was becoming more confident about being able to handle tricky situations without losing her temper, and noticing her successes. At our third meeting, when I asked the usual question 'What's going well?' she told me that a piece of her artwork had been chosen for a new display in the school's entrance foyer. As we were leaving the meeting room at the end of our meeting I asked her if she would show it to me. It was a framed pencil drawing on A3 paper. The whole sheet was covered with tiny, precise figures, in action on a sports field. There was so much attention to fine detail, it was breathtaking. I looked at her work. She stood beside me, not speaking.

I could have told her how impressed I was with the amount of work she had put into completing her picture, but instead I asked her a question:

Me: What is it about your work, that it was chosen to be put on display?

May: Well ... it is the best artwork I've ever done – but it's not finished. I asked if I could finish it, but it had to be put up this week.

She pointed out a small space in one corner where there were no tiny figures.

May: There ... see .... Not finished.

Me: Mmm ... The best artwork you've ever done. And it's been put on display. So what is it about you that could do work like this?

May: I don't know. Maybe that I really concentrate on the detail. When I draw something I know how I want it to look, and I just keep working at it until it's right.

Me: So if someone asked me about you, 'What is it about May, that she could produce work like that?' I might say, 'She's a person who will keep on working at something until it's right.' Is that true about you?

May: Yeah. I suppose. It's what I do with my football. I just practice and practice until it's right.

Me: Here's your job then, to notice yourself keeping on working at things till they're right, and what's going well, whatever you're doing at the time, and I'll ask you about it when we meet.

May: OK.

Me: See you next week, May. Bye.

COMMENT

In her school report, May was described as someone who would destroy her own work rather than let a teacher mark it, or even comment on it. This behaviour has been described an act of aggression tied up with the student's need to be in control, and gaining it by manipulating the teacher into getting angry or critical or shouting (Beadle and Murphy, 2013). Maybe it is true some cases, but how is the teacher to know if they are being directed by a student in need? Solution-support does not require any guesswork about what might be causing this sort of behaviour and is designed to provide the space for control and creativity to be shared between student and teacher in a balanced way. Self-efficacy goes together with self-assessment. For May, praise coming from the outside was too general to be useful because she might interpret it as a form of control. Her work was both good, detailed and carefully done, and bad because it was unfinished – and May was a perfectionist. Asking her about her own perspective on the work meant she could experience flow as an artist, her success realized from the inside, when she said it was the best artwork she had ever done. May's behaviour changed; she became the successful, confident student that she was, at her best. I met her several times in passing when I was in the school over the following months. She was always happy to talk and told me she was doing well.

Nearly a century ago the research of the psychologist Erik Erikson revealed the important role that self-validated success played in healthy development. The inquiry that May and I undertook on her accomplishment enabled her to check on its truth, and in that moment to recognize her peak performance, and to critique it without fear, in an internal, reflective process. This is a persistent theme, restated by Hattie (2009) who gave similar emphasis to the role of success. He referred to Levin's book *How to Change 5000 Schools* (2008), which argued that school improvement rests on improving daily teaching and learning practices, focused on a few key outcomes, putting effort into building capacity for improvement and building motivation by taking a positive approach. These requirements can be met by taking the solutions-focused approach actively promoting the positive and blocking the negative in a structured way. Talking about success and experiencing flow is motivating. Focusing on the resources that produce skilful action, asking the question 'What is it about you that you can do that?' supplies Levin's (2008) recommendation of taking a positive view.

Process: How can I do it?

Earlier in this chapter we looked at Wiliam's two key questions for teacher development (2012); having explored 'What is the task?' we will now look at the second question, 'How can I do it?'. This section is about action, what you can do in a practical way to grow and strengthen your confidence. Finding success in a teaching project that is suitably challenging, putting effort into making changes and getting feedback will help you in developing your confidence.

A concept in solution-focused thinking is that success in one area of activity tends to increase the likelihood of being successful in others, because perceived self-efficacy has a global effect, in the same way that Dweck's (2006) fixed or growth mindsets have global effects. This is demonstrated in several of the case stories in this book, where students improve their behaviour, the external goal, through their experience of success and flow with internal goals they identify for themselves. To reiterate, paying attention to your successes makes it more likely that you will have more successes to notice. If you think you are doing better, you probably will be. The experience of flow generates flow. If you model the habit of searching systematically for success, your students will perceive a greater sense of their self-efficacy too. Here, I will suggest a framework for selecting a project in the exercise below that you can start to use immediately. In Chapter 10 you will find a framework for solution-support and logic-modelled project planning.

EXERCISES

Keeping track of success

I recommend that you keep notes on your work relating to this book. I have found note-taking useful, particularly when I was taking my first steps down the solution-focused path. It can provide you with useful feedback, as you can track successes and changes in your practice and in your perception of self-efficacy. If this sounds rather formal, just think about it as miscellaneous jottings, a way of reflecting on your practice, and use it in any way that suits you. It also provides evidence of your professional development should you need it, with solution-focused scaling providing a good structure for conversation.

What's the worry?

In your notebook, write down five worries that you have at the moment, as a teacher. Only include those where change is possible in the fairly short term. Where you have a worry but you can't do anything about it, or you won't be able make any changes to improve it for a long time ahead, put it to one side for now, as part of the fixed landscape.

Selecting a suitable behaviour project

With the five possible projects where change is possible, mark them as either

- Controlled (Type C – requires a creative solution, negotiable, high challenge) or

- Automatic (Type A – has a rule-bound solution, non-negotiable, low challenge).

(Deci & Ryan, 1985; Pink, 2009)

Where a problem has a rule-based solution, mark it 'A' (automatic):

Example: Where there is a school rule for ending lunch-time play, in a primary school, students are taking a long time to come over and are not lining up quietly = A: low challenge, non-negotiable, suitable for extrinsic control through rewards.

Where a problem has a creative solution, mark it 'C' (controlled):

Example: When you ask questions of your class group, how can you make sure that everyone gets the chance to give an answer in a balanced, self-motivated way without your resorting to external control?

Working on the project

Type A projects are rule-based, so to address these make sure you know the relevant rule and that the students are clear about it and why the rule makes sense; for example, ending play-time quickly means getting to class on time to get to work, which means that everyone is safe and no-one gets left behind, and gives everyone a chance to show what they can do. Reinforce it with rewards if you choose to and if it is in the school culture to do so, but avoid 'if/then' rewards in favour of whole class 'now-that' rewards. Try this with a project you have marked with 'C' and take the solution-focused approach to it.

Structuring the project

Solution-support and solution-focused practice is open and creative by design, and it has a clear underlying philosophy and structure. If you are new to solution-focused working, it is recommended that you follow the structure closely at every opportunity in order to develop your expertise (Ratner et al., 2012: 244). Once you feel fluent, with the underlying

(Continued)

(Continued)

principles guiding your action, that is the time to adapt the model if it suits you and the students you teach.

In Chapter 10 you will find a number of resources to help you with the practical application of solution-support. In outline the framework is:

- What is my best hope for change?
- Suppose this worry is resolved, how will I know? What will I see happening differently that will tell me the worry is resolved?
- What might I have done differently for that to happen?
- What resources might I need, if any, to be able to do things differently?

If you want to structure this more formally, you can use the logic model, in which the steps are connected by the if/then question. It has four steps and starts with the intended outcome, in line with the solution-focused model, and works backwards from that in logical steps:

1. Outcome – the hoped for change resulting from the activity is happening in X) weeks or months from the start date.
2. Output – successful activity will produce this evidence of change.
3. Activity – in order to address the problem we will take this action, with these participants.
4. Resources/input – in order to accomplish the activities we need ...

Logically:

Resources – *if* we have these resources *then* we can do this activity.

Activity – *if* we do this activity involving these people *then* we can achieve this.

Output – *if* we achieve this output *then* we know we have achieved this.

Outcome –

Try this out with a real worry. Write your findings in your journal or talk the process through with a colleague if it seems appropriate.

Conclusion

This chapter has been about developing confidence in your practice as a teacher, particularly as newly qualified teachers consistently identify behaviour management as an area of practice where they need more support as they enter teaching. The bulk of the chapter has addressed the first of two developmental questions about content, 'What is the task?'.

I have introduced the ideas of flow and perceived self-efficacy as a foundation for thinking about the value and importance of recognizing success, and keeping a sustained focus on strength and resources as a way of developing your practice and your confidence.

It is important that you are in control of your own learning experience, to strengthen your internal motivation. Respecting this, and to answer the second question 'How can I do it?', I have suggested sorting the worries you might experience in your early days of teaching in order to deal with them appropriately. The first group, with rule-based solutions, are more straight-forward as they are non-negotiable and schools' policies and systems are written to deal with them. The second group have creative solutions, and solution-focused and logic-modelled outcome focused approaches may be useful to you here.

References

Bandura, A. (1994) 'Self-efficacy'. in V. S. Ramachaudran (ed.) *Encyclopedia of Human Behavior*, Vol. 4. New York: Academic Press. pp. 71–81.

Beadle, P. and Murphy, J. (2013) *Why Are You Shouting at Us? The Dos and Don'ts of Behaviour Management*. London: Bloomsbury.

Csíkszentmihályi, M. (1990) *Flow: The Psychology of Optimal Experience*. New York: Harper Perennial Modern Classics.

Davies, J. and Spencer, D. (eds) (2010) *Emotions in the Field: The Psychology and Anthropology of Fieldwork Experience*. Stanford: Stanford University Press.

Deci, E. and Ryan, R. M. (1985) *Intrinsic Motivation and Self-determination in Human Behaviour*. New York: Plenum.

Dweck, C. S. (2006) *Mindset: The New Psychology of Success*. New York: Random House.

Goleman, D. (2013) *Focus: The Hidden Driver of Excellence*. London: Bloomsbury.

Hattie, J. (1992) 'Influences on student learning'. Inaugural lecture, University of Auckland. Available at: https://cdn.auckland.ac.nz/assets/education/hattie/docs/influences-on-student-learning.pdf (accessed 3 November 2015).

Hattie, J. (2009) *Visible Learning: A Synthesis of over 800 Meta-analyses Relating to Achievement*. Abingdon: Routledge.

James, G. (2007) 'Finding a pedagogy'. Unpublished PhD thesis, University of East Anglia.

Kahneman, D. (2011) *Thinking Fast and Slow*. London: Macmillan.

Levin, B. (2008) *How to Change 5000 Schools*. New York: Harvard Education.

Lyubomirsky, S. (2007) *The How of Happiness: A Practical Guide to Getting the Life You Want*. London: Piatkus.

OECD (2008) 'The professional development of teachers'. France: OECD. Available at: http://www.oecd.org/berlin/43541636.pdf (accessed 3 November 2015).

Pink, D. H. (2009) *Drive: The Surprising Truth about What Motivates Us*. London: Riverhead.

Powell, S. and Tod, J. (2004) 'A systematic review of how theories explain learning behaviour in school contexts', in *Research Evidence in Education Library*. London: EPPI-Centre, Social Science Research Unit, Institute of Education.

Ratner H., George E. and Iveson, C. (2012) *Solution Focused Brief Therapy: 100 Key Points and Techniques*. Abingdon: Routledge.

Schaffer, O. (2013) *Crafting Fun User Experiences: A Method to Facilitate Flow*. London: Human Factors International.

Wiliam, D. (2012) *Embedded Formative Assessment*. Bloomington, IN: Solution Tree Press.

5

MAKING SENSE OF
BEHAVIOUR PROBLEMS

This chapter will give you the opportunity to:

- identify what type of behaviour problem you are dealing with and the problem-solving approach that fits them best

- make the most appropriate response

- know why you are doing what you are doing

- engage in the process of professional development which will lead to becoming a better problem-solver achieving improved outcomes for students

What is a problem?

'Problems are problems because they are maintained. Problems are held together simply by their being described as problems' (de Shazer, 1988). This quote from Steve de Shazer demonstrates an approach to problem-solving that we will touch on in this chapter.

A problem is an event which contains the possibility of change. If no change is possible then the event is a fact of life, an unavoidable occurrence, like having size nine feet or being older today than you were yesterday. When a change happens that alters the event in a desired direction, we call it the solution to the problem. When we do problem-solving work we tend to focus on the problem, assuming that the problem and the solution are directly connected to each other. If there is a possibility that a problem can be solved, the problem still exists. When a change happens and the solution is in place, the problem disappears.

Applying the problem-focused approach to behaviour, the focus of attention is on what has gone wrong. Getting to know about the behaviour problem comes first. Once it is fully known, the goal of any subsequent action is to eliminate the unwanted behaviour. This is the first step in conventional behaviour management in schools, finding out what the student cannot do. The next step is telling them to do it and checking to see if they have. The goal, such as 'staying in their seat for 80 per cent of all lessons over a two-week period' lays out what the student must do to achieve success. The strategies are tested and if they do not work the expert can suggest different ones – it is an experimental process. If this does not work, the problem is analysed in more detail. The assigned expert on behaviour, who might be a class teacher, a teaching assistant, a school manager or a behaviour specialist, questions the student and a range of other witnesses in order to develop a full understanding of the problem. The expert must ask all the correct questions about the event, who did what to whom and when, looking for signs of deficit and symptoms of disorder. This evidence collection may include information on the student's early life and their home circumstances.

The expert draws the evidence together, looks for a cause/effect relationship between stimulus and behaviour and suggests a strategy which may lead to the desired goal of eliminating the cause of the unacceptable behaviour. If a student's uncontrolled behaviour in class suggests that the student cannot control their emotions, an anger management course could be suggested. If this does not result in the behaviour being eliminated, another course could be suggested, but there are only a limited number of options available at school level. In problem-focused behaviour, management solutions are specified as end-goals for the student to work towards, not as part of the change process itself.

Steve de Shazer demonstrated through the observation of his own practice that the complicated and time-consuming problem-focused process can be reversed with striking results. In solution-focused work the process of change itself is structured by the intended solutions, and problems are mentioned only as the source of the success. Rather than being specified as end-goals, solutions are treated as being already in place, active and already happening to some degree. Students are characterized as having the strength, wisdom and experience to effect change. What is seen as a person's resistance to help in the problem-focused approach is reconceptualized as their best attempt at cooperation, something to be strengthened further rather than as a obstruction to be overcome. The solution-focused teacher walks alongside the student, working co-operatively while maintaining the necessary structure and boundaries to the work (de Shazer and Dolan, 2007).

Reframing problems in therapy and teaching

Psychotherapy has goals such as curing illness, changing personality traits or behaviour modification, which are not explicit goals of teaching.

However, what de Shazer noticed in the 1980s concerning psychotherapy's preoccupation with and focus on problems is equally true of the field of behaviour management today. Reframing a comment of de Shazer's problem-focused behaviour management developed a blind spot about the realization that there cannot be a concept of 'problem' unless the concept of 'solution' has already been developed (de Shazer and Dolan, 2007). The insight that de Shazer and his co-workers brought to addressing the limitations of this partial view of problem solving was that rapid change can be achieved by focusing on the solution. When the solution is happening the problem is gone, and when people come for support they are more interested in the problem going away than they are in exploring it in a great detail, before any suggestion of a way of getting rid of it is proposed. It is what people naturally want. This is equally true of both the student and the teacher, neither of whom at the start of the school day are hoping for failure.

If the direct route to the solution is possible, it makes sense to go that way, capitalizing on the self-motivation – what Pink (2009) calls the third drive – of the student hoping for change, to make it happen. The solution-focused approach takes an obvious short-cut by going directly to the solution. In working to change behaviour, the teacher is very often not an expert in the field, not through lack of interest but because of their lack of specialism and training. The solution-focused approach addresses this problem in two ways.

1. It engages an otherwise under-utilized resource: the self-motivation and self-expertise of the student.
2. It does not require a deep psychological and medical knowledge of human behaviour; it does require the person supporting the student to pay attention, to be curious and open-minded – and to be consistently solution-focused.

Behaviour problems – complicated or complex?

Some problems are complicated, by which I mean that the problem is made up of discrete parts that can be separated and identified, and which interact in predictable ways. To solve a complicated problem the appropriate focus is on the problem itself, analysing it to identify failed components, correcting or replacing the failure and assessing the outcome. For example, if a student made a persistent error in writing, then problem-focused problem-solving would be called for. The pedagogy to deliver the solution is directive, and does not require the student's active and imaginative cooperation, other than to carry out the teacher's directives to correct errors.

The place for problem-focused problem-solving

In the previous chapter, I introduced the idea of sorting the worries you might have to do with behaviour into those with non-negotiable rule-based solutions, with school's policies and systems written to deal with them, and those with negotiable solutions, the subject of creative work. If you stand back a little from behaviour to look across the range of issues that come up in school, you can see the utility of this approach. If a student in your class appears to have a difficulty of some kind that can be investigated by means of the sort of standardized assessments used by educational psychologists (e.g. dyslexia or dyspraxia), it is outside your remit as a teacher and you should refer to outside support. If your knowledge of the characteristic difficulties experienced by people with autism leads you to suspect this is causing barriers to be raised, hindering a student's participation and learning, this is a rule-based concern to be assessed by experts in the field. Returning to behaviour, rewards and clear reminders of rules and boundaries, but not punishments, can be used to reinforce non-serious, non-negotiable, rule-following behaviour without risking harm to students.

The place for solution-focused problem-solving

While some problems are complicated, other problems are complex, made up of interacting and unspecifiable elements, the sorts of problems that people meet in living their lives. There are no rules to refer to, the solution can only come about through creative problem solving, using an approach such as solution-support. The focus is on the solution, as 'how the world would be with the problem gone away'. Teaching for complex problem solving is through inquiry, focusing on the solution and instances of it already happening, and promoting reflective feedback for the student to maintain their control of the process, doing more of what works. In both cases the teacher has a clear role: in one case of the holder of knowledge and manager of the learning process; in the other case as the facilitator of the process holding the structure of the inquiry together.

Making sense of distress

Here is a real behaviour problem that was referred to me to solve. As you read the story, reflect on the nature of the problem, complicated or complex, and how my response fits it. Do not worry about the specifics of the solution-support process, we will come to those later. It is a quite long story, and I would ask you to stay with it, because it reveals the power of a student's agency, the third drive, in bringing about useful and healthy changes. You met Adam earlier in the book, in the letter his mother sent me.

Case story: Adam's story

What's the worry?

Adam is nearly 10 years old. It's halfway through the term, and he is missing a lot of school. His mum says that on some mornings he has been so distressed that she can't get him to leave the house. On other days, he gets as far as the school car park in her car, but refuses to get out. He cries and gets so distraught that she takes him home again. On the few days when he does go into school, she hands him over to the SENCO at the school door, who takes Adam to the classroom to help him to settle. But on some days he can't get there, and spends most of his time in the SENCO's room.

Adam's mother says she's tried everything, she's discussed the problems with the school and has talked to her doctor. The doctor has suggested a mental health assessment, because Adam's behaviour is beyond what the school is used to, and both they and his mother feel unable to deal with his problems. Adam's mum has been threatened with court action because she has failed to make him attend school, to 'overcome his school-refusal' as it is known. It is hard to understand what is causing Adam's problems, but there is clearly something seriously wrong. As the general practitioner suggested, the likely next step is to make a referral to the mental health experts to analyse the problem in order to come up with a diagnosis and some form of treatment for him.

Adam's school has a good reputation locally, and knows how to encourage reluctant children to come into school, to overcome their fears and worries about the big change involved in the move from home to school. The school had just occupied a brand new building, and the head teacher says she has all the resources needed to help children settle and learn. Adam's mum is very worried about him, and the school is looking for any help they and he can get.

I get a phone call from the head; could I help? I had worked in the school before, and my name had been mentioned in discussions in school about support for Adam. My office base was quite close to the school, so I arranged to come in when they called me, on account of his very irregular attendance.

The flow detectives

A few days later I meet Adam, his mother and the teaching assistant from his class, at 9.00 am. I suggest to Adam that our job in this meeting is to find out what he likes doing, and what he is good at. We make no mention of the problem at the start, and keep focused on moments of success that Adam recalls.

The conversation develops readily as I ask him for his ideas, and what he thinks his mum and the teaching assistant might notice about him when he's successful. I make notes on my pad, and every now and again show him the growing list of things I have written down. There is a happy mood in the room, and we talk for over half an hour. At the end of the time I sum up by counting out the number of things we have mentioned, and show him the notes again. I tell him I've got a job for him to do: to notice what's going well and tell me all about it when we meet next week, at the same time and place. We haven't mentioned the problem of his poor school attendance that brought us together.

It if works, do more of it

I compliment him on the noticing he's already doing, central to our meeting going so well. His mother compliments him on the way he's talked to three adults, trying his best. The teaching assistant compliments him on coming into school, and being ready to work today.

I ask him to remind me what his job is. He is not too sure so I remind him, and ask him what he has noticed about our meeting that has gone well. Then I ask him again to tell me what his job is, and this time he is clear about it and I compliment him on his accurate memory.

I ask him if he is going into class or going home now we've finished our meeting. He says he is going into class, we say goodbye, he hugs his mum and leaves with his teaching assistant.

Looking ahead and going in the right direction

After he has gone I ask his mum if she would like to know more about what I'm doing, and she says she would. I tell her that I am a teacher, and I'm doing something called solution-focused work with Adam, that I'm interested in Adam's successes, his strengths and resources. I'm also very interested in what he is hoping for, as far as school is concerned.

I tell her that I'm not looking to the past at what has gone wrong, but to the future where things will go right and that we'll meet again as a group in four weeks to review progress, and I'll be meeting Adam every week in school until then. She asks if she needs to do anything different, and I tell her that keeping on doing what she is doing is fine. She says she is going to pick Adam up at 3.00 pm, so his school day is a bit shorter and they can leave before things get busy at the official leaving time, 3.30 pm. I say goodbye to her and to the SENCO, and sign out of the school.

A week later I turn up for the planned meeting with Adam. I sign in at the school office and he walks in behind me with his mother and we say hello. As Adam and I walk to the meeting room, he starts telling me about what he's noticed going well. We meet for 20 minutes and use the 1–10 scale to structure our conversation. He says he had been into school every day, as something he's noticed going well. I ask him to do the same noticing task, and give him a compliment. I ask him if he'd like me to walk with him to the classroom, but he says he's fine and we say goodbye until next time. I watch him walk down the corridor and into his class. We haven't discussed any problems today.

The power of the third drive (Pink 2009)

A week later I am in school at 9.30 am, as we had arranged the previous week. When I get Adam from his classroom his teacher comes out too, to speak to me, and I ask Adam to go along to the meeting room.

Teacher: I'm a bit worried. Adam has been in school on time every day, but he was late yesterday, and I think it might be starting again. This happened before, he was OK at the start of term, then he started being late and then not coming in at all. I thought you ought to know.

Me: He's been in every day? That's good to hear. And thank you for telling me about yesterday.

Adam is sitting in his usual chair by the window, and he smiles at me as I enter. I ask him about what's going well, and he tells me about several things, but uppermost in his mind is that he's been in school every day and stayed until 3.00 pm, and he's been to his friend's house to play. I ask him if this is something different, and he says it is.

Adam: And yesterday I stayed all day, so I could do literacy.

Me: So you could do literacy. I see. On the other days you left at three, but yesterday you stayed all day, so you could do literacy. How come you did that?

Adam: I'm supposed to leave at three o'clock, but then I miss literacy. So I did my literacy, and then just stayed till the end of school. I had to come in at nine o'clock.

Me: Why was nine o'clock a good time to come in?

Adam: Because I had to stay to do my literacy.

Me: And how about today?

Adam: I don't have literacy today. But I'll stay till three thirty, and my mum will collect me.

Me: And what time will you be coming in to school tomorrow?

Adam: Eight thirty. That's what I do every day.

Me: And finish at three thirty. Is that right?

Adam: Yes.

Me: I'm just going to have a think, before I ask you another question. Is that OK?

Adam: Mmm ... yes.

I need to think through the story Adam has told me. He's been coming in every day at the correct time and leaving half an hour early, which meant he was missing out on his literacy lesson on the days it took place. He was supposed to be in school for six and a half hours. Because the literacy lesson ran through his agreed 3.00 pm end time, the school day had been shifted by 30 minutes so that he could stay until the end.

That way he could both attend for the agreed time, and do literacy. It made sense. And gradually lengthening a school day for students having problems in school is a commonly used strategy, which he was doing today. I turned back to Adam. A light had just come on – I had realized that Adam was working to a plan. But I didn't know where it had come from.

Me: Thanks for waiting for me, Adam. It seems to me that you've got a plan. Is that right?

Adam: Yes.

Me: And the plan was made by ...?

Adam: I don't know.

Me: OK, so the plan is for you to come in to school at the same time as all the other children, and leave at the same time, is that right?

Adam: Yes.

Me: What else is in the plan?

Adam: Coming to school with my friend.

I ask him to tell me more about the 'coming in to school' plan. He tells me that his mum walks him to school with his bike. On the way, he meets his friend, whose own mum also walks him in, with his bike. They meet near the school gates, ride into school together, park their bikes and go into class together. I tell him that seems like a good idea. He says he used to do that before.

The strength of autonomy

I draw a 1–10 scale in my notepad, with 1 meaning 'not coming into school' and 10 'in school every day' and ask him to mark it, to show where he is now. He marks the scale at 8. I ask him to mark where he was when we started our first meeting, he marks it at 2.

Me: So how come you have moved from 2 to 8?

Adam: Because I'm in school?

Me: So how come you could do that?

Adam: Because of the plan.

Me: Where do you hope you might be when I come in next week?

Adam: 10.

Me: So your job is to do the same as usual, keep on going with the plan, notice what's going well and I'll ask you about it next week. Now, for compliments.

Adam attended school every day, and when we reviewed at the end of the month, he felt we had finished our work and we agreed to end. We did compliments and task as usual and then I told him I was going to talk to his mum for a while.

After Adam had left to return to class, both his mother and the SENCO said they were worried that he might not be able to keep going, and that maybe I should carry on meeting him.

I said that since Adam felt we could finish, we should do so, because his confidence was a key to what had happened, and to support his decision would be for the best. I said I could understand their worry, and I would keep in touch with school to make sure they had the support they needed, and they could call me at any time if necessary.

I checked after one month and again after three months. Adam was attending and doing well in school. Adam's mother told me that actually the school had never known how desperate things had become before I got involved. She said that as soon as we started working together Adam changed; he stopped worrying about school, he began to sleep through the night, started asking to go to his friend's house to play, and going to the shops with her, as he used to do before the problems started.

COMMENT

The Plan

I was curious about where the plan had come from; it seemed to be a good one and was certainly useful to Adam. After the session when Adam first described it, I called in to the SENCO's room to check it out. I said Adam was following the plan, and did she know who had set it up. She said she hadn't heard of any plan. She knew that neither Adam's mother nor herself had put it together. She asked me if she could copy my notes showing Adam's scale, as she thought that scaling sounded like a useful idea. At the next meeting I asked Adam if the plan was his own idea. He said it was.

On an optimistic note

The conclusion to my work with students was normally thanks from teachers and parents and carers, and a brief written report in the student's file. I was very happy to conclude the work with a feeling of achievement and cheerful goodbyes.

After my work with Adam had concluded I had a conversation with his mother, who was interested in my very different approach to Adam's difficulties. She told me the scale of the change that her son had undergone as a result of the work we had done together. I mentioned to her that I hoped to be writing a book at some time, and it would be very valuable to have her impression of what we had achieved through the use of the solution-focused approach. Her note appears at the start of this book.

Conclusion

The story about Adam and his plan is a tale of problem solving and problems solved. Problem solving as an area of activity in schools is getting a good deal of attention these days. It is has a formal mention in the National Curriculum in England (DfE 2014) and has a long history as an aspect of mathematics in schools. Twenty years ago academics arguing for reform in teaching proposed that maths students should be engaged in the process of solving problems, rather than in just mastering skills and applying them mechanically, and this has spilled over into teaching generalized problem solving in schools today.

Traditionally, in the discussion of problem solving the distinction is made between the *acquiring* of information ('know-what' knowledge), typically by rote and repetition, and the *application* of knowledge ('know-how') in the solving of subject-related problems in problem solving.

In education the mathematical model of problem-solving is usually taken to represent problem solving in general. Solving behaviour problems has taken the same course and has come to dominate the field of behaviour management, with sometimes unfortunate outcomes for students. Standing back from the immediate problems experienced by Adam, and by his family and school in turn, and thinking about what kind of problem solving is most appropriate makes sense.

For a teacher to get to the situation where behaviour for learning happens by default takes considerable and sustained effort. The teacher has to balance the competing demands of the job coming from inside and outside the classroom, prioritize them and pour energy into those that emerge on top. Taking a problem-solving approach which will not lead to the hoped-for outcomes of improved behaviour makes an additional demand. This is clearly demonstrated in the story of Adam, where the problem-focused approach depending on external motivation did not bring him to a happier place, despite resources being poured into the effort.

How to make difference? Engage the solution-focused approach to problem solving and the third drive (Pink 2009), and who knows what is possible.

References

de Shazer, S. (1988) *Clues: Investigating Solutions in Brief Therapy*. New York: Norton.

de Shazer, S. and Dolan, Y. (2007) *More than Miracles: The State of the Art of Solution-Focused Brief Therapy*. Binghampton, NY: Haworth.

Department for Education (DfE) (2014) *The National Curriculum in England*. London: DfE.

Pink, D. H. (2009) *Drive: The Surprising Truth About What Motivates Us*. London: Riverhead.

6

BEING SOLUTION-FOCUSED
IN SCHOOL

This chapter will give you the opportunity to:

- know the structure of solution-support
- take your first steps in using solution-support in your own context
- know how to stay solution-focused when you are under pressure

How to do solution-support work

Belief, choice and mindset

When you approach a student whose behaviour is causing problems, you can believe what you want about them, why they are behaving this way, what is in it for them, what motivates them. As a free agent you can choose what to believe, you can change your mind and change your mindset. Your beliefs underpin your mindset, which directs your actions. You can believe that students are successful, resourceful and hopeful, or that they are failing, lacking resources and aimless. You can believe that they are motivated only by their need for the biological basics, or by carrots and sticks. Or you can believe that this is last-century thinking and that their main motivator is what Pink (2009) called the 'third drive', building on what Deci (1972) described as a tendency that people have to seek out novelty and challenges, to develop and exercise their capabilities, to explore new territory and to learn. Pink's (2009) third drive is energized by the student's need for:

- autonomy – being self-directed, having a sense of self-control
- experience of being expert (mastery) – getting better at doing something that matters.

What about discipline?

Does Pink's (2009) call for attention to be paid to the third drive mean that carrots and sticks are consigned to the compost heap? As a teacher, you are expected to be able to discipline students when necessary, and to do it intelligently. Discipline, or to be more accurate in the context of teaching, external discipline, has its place in managing behaviour, provided its limitations are clearly understood. In managing routine, unchallenging, rule-based tasks, the reward component of external discipline can provide a small motivational boost, without any harmful side-effects. The punishment component of external discipline can interrupt off-task behaviour, but it can also have harmful side-effects unless it is applied within strict guidelines. It does not lead to new learning, so its effect is temporary and short term.

Beyond discipline

Why bother going beyond carrots and sticks when they are very easy to apply, and teachers are consistently being told to use them? For two reasons:

- Because reward and punishment have seriously limited utility for you and the students you are trying to help. If behaviour does not change through the conditioning effects of reward and punishment you can easily get stuck, and that is a stress inducing situation for all parties.
- It is important to take every opportunity to teach students new thinking and new skills. Rewards and particularly punishments do not reliably do this, whereas by modelling and using the third drive students can learn important new skills in the process of reaching the goal of changed behaviour.

Incidentally, as a teacher becoming familiar with the concepts and practice of solution-support as a form of inquiry learning, you will be able to apply it in other areas of the curriculum where students are working on creative tasks.

'If you want to get to there, you shouldn't start from here'

Essex country wisdom, Anon

Non-teaching professionals working in education tend to focus on the nature of problems to attempt to resolve the difficulties that students experience. They are trained in this approach, and it serves the needs of many students who experience well-defined difficulties. As classroom teachers we too receive some training in behaviour and behaviour problems, as generalists rather than specialists, and know enough to follow the generally accepted problem-focused rules. The behaviour policies you come across in schools will be based on the same thinking. Problem-focused problem solving, problem analysis and the behaviourist, experimental approach to correcting behaviour go together. When I first took a full-time interest in behaviour and behaviour management I did not know that there was another way to go about the work, as a teacher. I merely did more of what had gone before.

Whose solution?

Solution-focused thinking is not problem-focused thinking with positive spin. It does not ignore problems, it treats them respectfully and differently. It is based on different assumptions.

Solution-support is underpinned by three beliefs about the student:

1. The student has a *successful past*; the change they are hoping for is already happening, and it can be found if you look for it.
2. They are *resourceful*, and they have the capacity to make changes.
3. They are *hopeful* about their preferred future.

When you are doing solution-focused work, it is important to have these three beliefs firmly in mind because they will keep you aiming at solutions when the going gets tough.

The solution-support ground-rules are, in no particular order:

- The student is the expert in themselves.
- Students are doing their best, even when it does not look like it.
- If a problem does not have a solution, it is not a problem; do not worry about it now.
- Investigate the solution, not the problem.
- Unwanted behaviour is simply something to be changed through new learning.
- The smallest solutions can collapse the biggest problems.
- Something is already working; find out it what it is and do more of it.
- You can only know what you are told; listen carefully.
- Be curious.

You might find it useful to note in these in your journal to prompt you when you are in conversation with a student. I did when I started out.

In any particular situation in teaching, if you choose to adopt the three beliefs and observe the ground-rules above, you can do solution-focused work.

Conventionally, behaviour management starts with a problem and stays with it, with questions like 'What's gone wrong?', 'How did that happen?' and so on. The purpose is for the teacher to get sufficient information to decide what needs to be changed and how to do it. Solution-support starts with the problem too, as the 'something to be changed', but moves on to the solution, what it is that might be changed to make a difference, from the student's perspective. When the student knows where they are hoping to get to, it becomes more likely they will get there. Solution-support does not deny that the problem exists. Far from it, it treats a problem as real to the person to whom it is causing difficulties, but it is hard to describe clearly because one problem is usually linked to others in complex ways.

Problem-free talk – a big idea

Problem-free talk is important for setting the solution-focused present, and for what comes next. The talk tends to be light-hearted, about things that go well and are fun. Follow your curiosity, there are no rules about where this conversation goes, other than it is the student's story not yours in the telling. If you notice you are about to change track and go to your story, resist the temptation, take a breath and get back to the student's story. For example, if the student brings something up that you know a lot about and you feel yourself about to add something new to add to their story, coming from your experience, just simply *do not say it*. I was doing some work for the Connexions service, aimed at getting more students into education, employment or training. A student told me her best thing was walking her dog.

Me: Tell me more about that.

Student: We've got a golden retriever.

            ⌈I am thinking: 'I had a retriever. Lovely dog.'⌉

Me: Tell me more about your dog.'

Student: She's very pale blonde.

            ⌈I think: 'So was mine.'⌉

Student: She's called Lyn.

⌈I think: 'That's amazing, my dog was called Lyn too!'⌉

I am nearly bursting to tell her, but it is not my story that is important here, it is her's. I remember the rule, and ask her to tell me more about the walk instead. It preserves her position as the storyteller, the resourceful expert in herself, and maintains the all-important balance of power in the relationship.

COMMENT

It important to respect the student's story, in view of the third-drive condition of autonomy. Try this out whenever you get an opportunity, ask a student what is their best thing, stand back and try to prevent yourself taking over. If you practice, you will get to be good at it.

Finding the exception

Although it might seem that a student always has a certain problem in a certain context, the ground-rule on exceptions to the probem tells us that this is not true. There will be an exception, a time when everything was set for the problem behaviour to emerge, and it did not. Finding the exception is a very powerful experience, for both the supporter and the supported. It breaks a rule and proves the existence of the solution already happening. You can rely on an exception being there; finding it is sometimes hard work, but it is well worth the effort as it resets the growth mindset of the student. In my experience it is always treated as a completely rational question by students I have worked with, and they set about looking for the exception quite casually, as they had done earlier in looking for what they like doing.

You will meet Val later in this chapter. Here's a brief exchange from her story:

Me: Let's go back to our work project, Val. Not get involved in other people's arguments – that's what you thought might make a difference. Tell me a time when things were going as usual in school, you were around other people as usual and you could have got involved in their arguments. And you didn't!

Val: I don't know. ..... Last week? In Tech.

Me: So what did you differently?

Val: Got on with my work.

Me: How come you didn't get involved?

Val: I don't know. I just did my work.

COMMENT

When I started doing solution-focused work I was doubtful about this 'Tell me a time when ...' question. It flew in the face of all the evidence I had been given about students, 'This student always misbehaves in unsupervised time'. I had been told that Val always got involved in arguments, all over the school. However, in the solution-focused world we know that there will have been a time when the problem that the student brought with them did *not* happen, and the solution happened instead. As I gained confidence I learned to ask this question in a straightforward way. When a student is asked 'Tell me a time when ...', it needs some thinking about if their recent past seems to them to be filled with failures. They have to block the failure-map, allow the success-map to operate and pay attention to it. It might take some time for the student to recall the exception. They may never have heard a question like this before.

A solution-focused idea is that there is as much information in the question as there is in the answer. Having asked a question, leave it alone. If you were to ask another question, the information in the new question will interfere with the information in the original question, and make it more difficult for the student to pay attention to it. It is best to give time for the student to answer, even if it seems a long time to you. You can tell if they are engaged in the process by all the signs, verbal and non-verbal, that they give. If they look stuck after two minutes you could ask 'Is that question OK for you?'.

If the student says 'It's OK', keep quiet.

If the student says she needs help, ask exactly the same question again and wait. When the answer comes back, I often experience what I call in Chapter 3 a 'flash-flow'. The foundation for change is established, the solution-map is activated and through reliving the 'time when ...' it becomes possible for the student to strengthen it further by paying attention towards it and away from the blocked problem-map. As the solution strengthens, the problem weakens.

Autonomy and feedback – the conditions for flow

An outcome of successful teaching is the development of students' autonomous thinking and action. For a student to think about where they hope to get to and where they are now on the path, and what they are going to do next, scaling is very useful. Scales in solution-support are designed to provide a reflective surface, and it is important to recognize the difference between problem-focused scaling and solution-focused scaling in order to use them appropriately. Behaviour improvement plans often include problem-focused scaling. If a student is causing problems by fighting in the playground, the plan might specify something like: 'Achieve six out of ten outside morning playtimes over the next two weeks without having to be removed for fighting.' The student would be given this target to bring their attention to what was not wanted. I call this the 'find out what he can't do and tell him to do it' approach. The assumption is that this would be sufficiently motivating to make them behave better, and it quantifies their achievement if it happens, but it does not promote autonomous action on the part of the student.

Case story: Solution-support in action

Here is a case story that explores the structure of solution-support, with a student in secondary school. Val was starting her last year in school. She was described as always having been disruptive in school, joking and disrespectful when she should have been working, noisy and off-task in class. The effects of her behaviour on other students was an issue as the year group were moving towards their exams, and despite the school using their best efforts to encourage her to change, or to control and discipline her, she seemed unteachable. She was frequently sent out of class, her teachers concentrating on her peers who were getting on with their work.

I was called in to work with her when permanent exclusion had become imminent, and the school was prepared to make one last attempt to include her. I offered to do the work within the framework of a pastoral support programme (PSP). These are generally problem-focused, using SMART (smart, measured, achievable, relevant and time-bound) targeting and review, with a large number of individuals and agencies involved. I was invited to attend PSPs using this format, but found the external goal setting unsatisfactory, even when a PSP pro forma was presented as having solution-focused elements. I developed and used a fully solution-focused PSP, running for eight weeks with fortnightly meetings. Val's mother, Mrs. West, was invited to the all the meetings, but subsequent meetings were between Val and myself, as her mother was unable to attend due to work commitments.

Introduction to the session

I started by setting the scene, briefly setting out the principles of the solution-focused approach to Mrs West and Val about the principles of solution-focused work, that Val and I would be looking forward to where she was hoping to get to, rather than looking backwards at what had gone wrong. She said she was pleased about that because she was in so much trouble in school and there was no point in going over it all again. I said Val and I would meet every two weeks until half-term and then the four of us would review progress together.

> *Me*: Val, do you know what permanent exclusion means?
>
> *Val*: Mmmm ... Not really.
>
> *Me*: You will have to leave school and you won't be allowed back – not even onto school grounds to meet your friends. Unless things change of course. Would you be interested doing some work on that, on where you want to get to this year?
>
> *Val*: Er ... OK.

COMMENT

Introducing the idea that we would be focusing on Val's successful future rather than the problems that had occurred in the past was the first step. A straightforward description of Val's situation, to make clear the purpose of the work and that it represents a real challenge came next. A student may not realize that they are in serious trouble because from their point of view they are not doing anything different, just behaving, or misbehaving, as usual. There was the clear suggestion that we could work together for a better outcome. The language keeps the power balanced, inviting Val to work rather than instructing her to do so.

Best hope

Next I asked Val for her best hope for the meeting.

> *Me*: Suppose we did some work together that was useful to you, what is your best hope for the work – what would it be about?
>
> *Val*: Err ... Not getting kicked out?

Me: OK, so suppose that happened and you didn't get kicked out, what would happen instead?

Val: Stay in school till the end of the year?

COMMENT

A solution-focused belief is that people are hopeful. Val states her own hope as an attainable goal, with a long-term outcome of staying in school. To do this she has to think it through, so the pace of our conversation is important, asking a question and the waiting quietly for her reply. I ask her to convert her first negative goal into a positive one, because you can't not do something; the goal becomes a positive action.

The project

Me: So if we did some work together and as a result you stayed in school until the end of the year, that would be useful to you. Is that right?

Val: Yeah.

Me: So suppose you did stay in school until next summer, what might you do a bit differently for that to happen?

Val: Not get involved in other people's arguments?

Me: What would you do instead of getting involved in other people's arguments?

Val: Errr ... get on with my work.

COMMENT

A solution-focused belief is that people are resourceful. In common with many other teaching and learning situations in school, solution-support is set up as a project requiring work, in this case with a self-selected learning goal. A principle in solution-support is that some things are within the control of the student and can be changed, and these are set against the background of all those things that are relatively fixed: the behaviour policy, teacher's opinions, time, being a teenager and so on. Asking Val to reflect on this and to come up with a challenging and attainable project for herself, places her as the resourceful expert on herself. She makes the same negative-to-positive shift in focus as before, blocking the problem mind map and promoting the creative mindset. Once the project is defined, subsequent solution-support conversation maintains this block, and strengthens the success mind map.

Problem-free talk

Me: I'd like to ask you about something different. What's your best thing? What are you good at, what do you like doing?

Val: Nothing.

Me: I mean something you're good at a bit, you like doing a bit maybe?

Val: Nothing. My teachers told me I was shit in primary school when I was six and I am.

Me: Mmm .... Nothing. When you were six? That sounds tough for you. 'Nothing' is a useful answer. It tells me to ask you that question another way. Suppose I asked your Mum – and she sees you a lot guess, sees what you do, she knows you best – to tell me something that you like doing, maybe just now and then, and you do a good job at it – what might that be? Have you got something in mind, Mrs West? That Val does OK?

Mrs West: Mmm ... yes.

Me: What do you think that might be Val, what might your mum be thinking about?

Val: Helping her with the cooking?

Me: Helping her with the cooking – I wonder if that's what your mum was thinking of. Shall we ask her? Was that what you had in mind, Mrs West?

Mrs West: Well, actually I was thinking about something else but yes ... you do help me and you're good at cooking.

Me: So what is it about you that makes you good at cooking, Val? How come your mum can say that?

Val: Careful at weighing out the flour and butter and stuff?

Me: Is that right, Mrs West?

Mrs West: Yes.

Me: And your mum's got something else in mind too. Can we ask you about that in a few minutes, Mrs West? OK, so what about you, Val, what else do you like doing, you're good at?

Val: Jokes?

Me: What tells you you're good at jokes?

Val: I make people laugh in class.

Me: So what is it about you that makes you good at jokes?

Val: I don't know – I just see things in a funny way?

COMMENT

This part of the conversation shifts the student's thinking towards competence and success, and away from failure.

> *Me*: What's your best thing? What are you good at, what do you like doing?
>
> *Val*: What do you mean, in school or at home or what?
>
> *Me*: Anywhere, school, home, with friends, on your own —your best thing.

This is called problem-free talk and is a good way to get to know someone and what makes then happy, and begin to explore their strengths and resources. Even students you know quite well may tell you about things you never suspected. A student in primary school told me he was a cook and could make a soufflé, a difficult thing to do. His head teacher had no idea that this was his passion, and he had talked about it in answer to such a simple question. Once you get started, be led by your curiosity, follow the story that is being told to you and be guided by it in asking questions. To make sure it is the student's story and not your own taking over, remember that you cannot know your next question until you have heard the previous answer. As you hear about successes, at a good moment ask a question about the student's strengths and resources.

Initially, in asking Val to talk about success, her long-established habit of noticing failure blocked her thinking about success. I was asking her to give herself a compliment, in a way, and she found it hard to do. Directly reflecting her own language tells her I am paying attention and not marginalizing her previous experiences. My belief is that she is doing her best, so when she said 'Nothing', I took that as her best answer to the question I had asked her. My job was to find a better question, and asking about a third-party perspective is often useful. Asking her what her mum might have been noticing engaged Val's imagination and creativity. I had no predesigned plan for problem-free talk and Val was free to look for successes wherever she wanted to go, without external control, given that we stayed within accepted boundaries, because successes and self-efficacy are interconnected in a person's mind.

Finding the exception to the rule

Me: Let's and go back to the project, Val. We've got about 10 minutes left. 'Get on with my work' – that's what you thought might make a difference. So this is something to think about – tell me a time when things were going as usual in school, you could hear other people arguing and you could have got involved in their argument as usual – and you didn't, you just got on with your work.

Val: I don't know ...

Me: Hmmm ... you don't know? Well, suppose you did. Even though you said you don't know, suppose you did know a time when you could have got into someone else's argument, and you didn't. Tell me about that.

Val: Last week? In Tech?

Me: What did you differently then?

Val: Got on with my work.

Me: How come you could do that?

Val: I don't know – I just did.

Me: So that time in Tech you just did it. Is that right?

Val: Yeah.

Me: What would your teacher have noticed about you that was different?

Val: Well, I always get involved with other people and I didn't, I just kept my head down, did my work.

COMMENT

Although it might seem that a student always has a certain problem in a certain context, a ground-rule tells us that this is not true. There will be an exception, a time when everything was set for the problem behaviour to emerge, and it does not. Finding the exception is a very powerful experience, for both the supporter and the supported. It breaks a rule and proves the existence of the solution already happening. You can rely on an exception being there; finding it sometimes takes some hard work, but it is well worth the effort. It resets the growth mindset of the student. In my experience it is always treated as a completely rational question by students, and they set about looking for the exception quite readily, as they had done in looking for what they like doing. It is a direct question, 'Tell me a time when (the problem) did not happen', worded appropriately. In the reply is evidence of the solution already happening, and it turns a key. Once you both know the solution, even though it might be the smallest indication, it is a simple next step to do more of what is working.

When I asked Val the exception question, she said 'I don't know', a straightforward answer I hear often. By shifting the question away from hard reality and into creative imagination, 'Suppose you did know?', I have found that the student will always find the answer, and Val was able to find an exception. Remember, pace is important: ask the question and wait for the answer while the student is working on it.

Scaling

Me: OK, Val, I'd like to ask you a different question. On this scale where 10 on the scale is you doing whatever you need to stay in school and 1 is you doing what it takes for getting kicked out, where would you put yourself now, on the scale?

I gave her my pencil. She hovered it over the line, settled near midway and made a mark.

Me: What number would that be?

Val: Six.

Me: So how come you're already at 6 and not at 1? I mean 6 is over half way to 10 and 10 is you at school for the whole year. What are you doing already that puts you at 6?

Val: Doing my work?

Me: Doing your work puts you at 6 now. When we meet in two weeks, where do you hope you might be on the scale? Maybe the same place, maybe changed a bit?

Val: Seven.

Me: So what might you be doing to get nearer to 7 over the next two weeks.

Val: Doing my work.

COMMENT

Scaling the project makes goal setting and change visible. I use a horizontal 1–10 scale. This is not designed to be an objective scale, its purpose is to represent the student's subjective understanding in some way that enables us to talk about it without the need for analytical searching. It illustrates the student's best hope for change, their goal, and the process of change in real time. I intentionally do not use preprinted forms for solution-support, always starting with a blank sheet of paper as a sign that I have nothing preplanned, and asking the student to make their own marks on the scale.

Scaling is often the most memorable feature of the work from the student's point of view. You should think carefully about what 10 represents and then what 1 stands for, as the scale must clearly represent the project. In this case Val has said what she needs to do is to stay in school and 10 represents her achieving the goal; 1 is Val doing whatever it takes to get excluded. I offer students a scale drawn on paper, drawn by themselves, for them to take away when they go as a real object. I do not require them to bring it with them when we meet again. Younger students particularly find this a useful memory aid, until they internalize the scale. With the very youngest students I would ask their closest supporter in class to be involved in the making and use of the scale, as an additional resource.

Task

Me: Val, I'm going to ask you to do something. It's to notice things going well in school, things that are telling you that you are at 6 or maybe even nearer to 7 on your scale. No writing, just notice and remember. That's your job. When we meet next time I'll ask you what you've noticed.'

COMMENT

I make the task as non-specific as possible, as I hope Val will notice successes I do not know about and that may be highly significant to her. The task relates to the scale, which Val can carry out of the room in her imagination. The task makes the project a continuous piece of work that is the student's responsibility to keep doing. Val will get feedback internally by relating this project to her scale, and externally the next time we meet.

Compliment

Me: I'd like to give you a compliment on the work you've done today. You've really paid attention, I know that because you've answered all the questions I've asked you. That's my compliment to you.

I asked the Deputy Head to compliment her, and Mrs West to do so too, who said she thought the way Val spoke showed that she could do more than mess about in school. I asked Val to compliment herself, and she said it was for being at 6 on the scale. I closed the meeting three minutes late.

COMMENT

Compliments in solution-support are based on evidence. They are not intended to be equivalent to praise and reward, but offer another opportunity for reflective assessment of resources and strengths. Often students who were unused to giving and receiving compliments at the start of our work, by the end would do so routinely, sometimes spontaneously complimenting me on my work with them.

REFLECTION

Check the conversation so far against Pink's (2009) third drive conditions of autonomy, the experience of being an expert (mastery) and purpose.
What do you notice about Val's self-motivation?

The follow up meeting

'Seven,' Val said as she came into the meeting room. We sat down.

Me: How do you know that?

Val: Because my teachers have told me, one of them told me she's a bit amazed that I've been doing my work.

Me: What else tells you that you are at 7?

We continue the inquiry into her success, looking for evidence. What might her mum, the deputy head, the head teacher, her friends have noticed that would tell them that things had changed, that she was just getting on with her work?

I ask Val for her best hope for the next two weeks. She says it is to be at 8. I offer her a task.

Me: Your task is exactly the same as last time, to notice what's going well for you. When we meet next time, I'll ask you what you've noticed.

I compliment her on the work she has done over the last two weeks to get to 7 on the scale. I ask her to compliment herself and we end the meeting after 20 minutes.

COMMENT

Follow-up meetings are often over in a few minutes as the agenda is clear: 'When we meet next time, I'll ask you what you've noticed.' Very often a student will start the meeting off before I've said a word, as they have carried their scale in their mind and are eager to tell me about the progress they have made. Again, this is their subjective assessment and I am not interested in trying to objectify it. It is an indicator of change. The noticing task frees them up to take the project into any context they choose, at home, at school, in leisure time.

Those bloody teachers

I was at the local Pupil Referral Unit (PRU) one afternoon. Val had come in for a session to fill a gap in her school timetable, and we passed in the corridor.

Val: Those bloody teachers!

Me: Oh, what about those teachers?

Val: One of them said, 'Oh come on Val, you're going to have stay on to sixth form!'

In solution-focused work we know that change is constant and can happen anywhere, due to the connectedness of people in communities. As Val changed, so did people around her, notably her teachers as they became more aware of her potential to succeed. This makes solution-support much more broadly effective than other goal-directed work intended to change the behaviour of the student alone. It makes the job of change-making simpler too. In solution focused terms it is known as the ripple effect, where change in one part of a system that promotes change in other parts.

As recommended, the PSP ran for one term. At Christmas time, at the final review, with Val and Mrs West, the deputy head said things had improved to such an extent in school that Val was no longer at risk of permanent exclusion. Mrs West said she had noticed a marked change for the better at home too. Val said teachers became easier on her and she was getting on with her work in class. She agreed that our work together was complete and she would not need further support.

Throughout the term, I did not speak to anyone in school other than the head teacher about Val's project and the PSP. Val's teachers did not get reports of what we were doing and there were no multiagency PSP meetings. Through the remainder of the year, the deputy head let me know from time to time that Val was doing well, and she completed Year Eleven successfully. In the autumn she got a job on the school's domestic staff, working with her mother who had been a cleaner there for years. So she did stay on after all. Bloody teachers.

A hopeful perspective

I talked to the deputy head at the end of the year, after Val had completed her exams. He told me he had been using the solution-focused approach himself. He said that 'A main difference was that this approach to teaching behaviour had given them the confidence to believe there is an answer. There's a way forward, whereas perhaps in the course of a day they get het up with what's just happened, or the fact that punishment will catch up.'

He felt it put the necessary work into the context of looking forward, to where students are going rather than where they have been. It encouraged them to think beyond themselves in a sense of 'Where do I now go with this, how can things be better?'.

About Val, he said:

DH: You've only got to look at how much better she feels about herself. Her confidence and the self-esteem, she clearly didn't have in September, and the success she feels, she has achieved by getting through the year. I think it was the target and encouragement that you offered, that always looked to the next step, that made that possible. And not go down the same dead ends. Everybody needs to know how to do that.

Another case story

Here is a second case story for you to read, this time involving a much younger student. While reading it look for:

- the solution-support structure of problem-free talk, best hopes question, exception finding, scaling, task and compliment;
- the third-drive conditions of autonomy, experience of being expert.

Six-year-old Greg was often hurting other children in school, particularly at play times, and the head teacher was receiving complaints from parents of other children about it. His class teacher told me she felt deskilled by this serious and articulate child, who did not seem to understand about playing and hurting. She looked exhausted. The head teacher said she was under pressure to exclude him because they could not see a way to help him and maybe he would do better in another school. She had never permanently excluded a child before.

My first meeting with Greg, his teacher and his mother was filled with problem-free talk, as was the second; this time just Greg and me, talking about his successes and strengths. Greg had an encyclopaedic knowledge of local coaches and a great memory for their names, numbers and makes. He told me a lot about them. Coming into school for the third meeting, as I walked up the long corridor towards his classroom I could hear loud crying, and saw a girl with sand on her head and Greg nearby with a large plastic box in his hands.

'You've come at the right time,' his teacher said as she took the crying girl into her room. I went with Greg to our small meeting room looking out onto his classroom, the corridor and the sand.

Me: Good morning, Greg. It's nice to see you again.

Greg: Good morning, Geoffrey James.

Me: I saw you and the little girl and the sand on the floor. What were you doing, to be at your best?

Greg: I put half the sand on her head.

Me: I see – you put half the sand on her head. Tell me a bit more about that. How was that you being at your best?

Greg: She's got long hair, so I put half.

Me: She's got long hair and you put half the sand on her head. So how come you were doing your best?

Greg: She isn't allowed to wear the rings and she's got long hair over them, so I only put half the sand.

Me: Ah, I see. So how come you could put half the sand and not put all the sand on her head? What is it about you that you could do that?

Greg: I choosed.

Me: So you choosed and you poured half the sand. Is that right?

Greg: Yes.

A common rule in schools is 'no jewellery'. This girl had earrings which broke the rule, but you could not see them because they were covered by her long hair. To Greg this meant a half-broken rule.

Maybe he seemed to be out of control, but actually he had only put half the sand on her head, probably not too easy to do as the dry sand came pouring out of the box. He had told me about an exception, about a time when he kept control of himself, even though it did not look like it from the outside. Having found the exception we could use it to develop a scale. I drew a line in my notebook and numbered it 1 to the left and 10 to the right. The resource he had demonstrated was choosing.

Me: On this scale, 10 is you choosing and 1 is you not choosing. When you poured the sand, where were you on the choosing scale?

I gave him my pencil and he studied the scale line. He marked the scale at 5.

Me: So what did you do to be at 5 and not at 1?

Greg: I choosed to pour half the sand.

Me: And when I ask you about the scale next week, do you hope you'll be at 5 on the choosing scale, or somewhere else?

Greg: I'll be at 10.

COMMENT

Being curious about what happened in the corridor with the sandbox, and having an open mind about how it might be explained, led to a good outcome for Greg. It requires discipline to be able to see past the obvious explanation when something goes wrong and the solution-focused approach can provide the necessary structure. From the outside it seemed that Greg was behaving in his usual hurtful way, but from his perspective he was working hard at what he was good at – being responsible, helping to enforce school rules, making choices – and he described it to me. It was not simply one child attacking another for no apparent reason. Greg had a logical explanation for his action, and it led to the recognition of his ability to make a choice in a tricky situation.

The important things to Greg were that his strength – being able to choose – was recognized; he could set his own goal for change; he could recognize his own success; he was half-way to his goal already and by doing more of the same thing he hoped to reach it. Greg's autonomy was supported by seeing him as a resourceful person. I did not give him any advice, nor did I have to spend time trying to analyse what caused his behaviour, we simply moved straight to the solution, how the world would be with the problem gone.

From my point of view, the scale gave us a means of communication to talk about things that might otherwise have been difficult to express, given that it was performance, know-how, that he was describing. And know-how is very difficult to put into words at any age, let alone at 6 years old.

Assessing strengths and recognizing needs

Within a few days staff were confident enough in the changes Greg had made to let him play outside again, and he responded by choosing to play safely. I talked to the educational psychologist on my team about Greg's strengths, about his encyclopaedic knowledge of coaches and his unusual clarity about rule-following, and whether she might talk to his mother about further assessment. I was told that in fact he had already been referred for autistic spectrum disorder assessment, although it was not in his notes and I had not been informed before I went in to school to meet him.

At the fifth meeting to review progress, I asked Greg if we had finished our work and he said he would like to carry on meeting. We had another five meetings and agreed to end on the fifth. He was diagnosed with Asperger syndrome some time later, and continued making good progress in school.

When he was 10, he asked his mother if he could see me again and I met him in his primary school. He wanted to work on the transition to high school, which he was worrying about. We had five meetings over a month with a successful conclusion.

When he was 15, I had a message that he would like to meet up again. We met twice in his high school, he remembered clearly the solution-focused process, he was still choosing and still interested in coaches. He wanted to check out where he was, with the exams coming up, and said he always found our work useful. We did not meet again.

Doing the work, making changes, setting the task

Returning to Greg and the sandy corridor:

Me: And when I ask you about the scale next week, do you hope you'll be at 5 on the choosing scale or somewhere else?

Greg: I'll be at 10.

Me: I'll ask you about that next week. It's nearly time to finish now. I'm going to give you a job to do. It's about noticing. I'll show you what I mean. Tell me something you can notice in this room.

The small meeting room was used for one-to-one teaching and the walls were covered with posters and charts and numbers, very colourful and varied. Greg pointed out things he noticed.

Me: That's it exactly – noticing. Now I'm going to ask you to do something. I would like you to notice when you are choosing. Like when you chose to pour half the sand. Can you tell me your job?

Greg: To be good?

Me: That would be fine, but next week I am going to ask you what have you noticed about your choosing? So your job is to notice yourself choosing, at school, at home, anywhere. What's your job?

Greg: To notice choosing.

Me: That's right. What are you choosing right now?

Greg: Talking to you?

Me: Exactly.

COMMENT

The time available for meeting always seems too short and it is always possible to do something useful provided you keep focused. In a class of 30 students it is only possible to commit a few minutes a week to talk to each one. Where there is a more urgent need for behaviour teaching, as in Greg's case, it might be possible to use the time which would have been spent fire-fighting doing creative solution-support work instead.

One difference between problem-focused instruction and solution-focused inquiry is in how the time *between* the direct student–teacher work is spent. Greg had the open task of noticing himself making choices, in other words being reflective, thinking about thinking, noticing his success and other people's reactions to his good choices. He could do this any and all of the time and experience flashes of flow through the exercise of his own skills and strengths. Looking forward to our next meeting, when he could talk about success, gave him a short-term goal, with the means of achieving it lying within his own control. The combination of the graphical representation of the process as a scale and the simplicity of the self-selected goal seems to stabilize the task from the student's perspective.

The meaning of autonomy

I met a 6-year-old for a first meeting in mid-July, just before the long summer holiday, with his teacher and his grandparents who were fostering him. Using exactly the same structure as with Greg, at the end of our first meeting I set him his task. He had scaled himself at 5 for walking rather than running around school, and hoped to be at 7 when we met next time, after the summer holidays. I asked him to look out for what was going well, and I said I would ask him about it the next time we met.

We met again in mid-September. I was waiting for him when he came into school with his grandparents. He walked straight up to me and said, 'I'm at 7!' in a proud voice.

I was impressed with his memory for the task and for his progress in getting to 7 and I told him so. His grandparents said he had been looking forward to our meeting, so he could tell me about it. This persistence with the task and students walking into the room and telling me about where they have got to has happened repeatedly. At first it surprised me, but now I know I can rely on the student working away at their own successful change, merely using me as mirror to reflect their success back to them, while the old problem habit disappeared to be replaced by the success habit.

Conclusion

The origin of solution-support lies in a talking therapy. I treat solution-support as a talking, teaching approach and do not incorporate elements of play or art or drama, as do some others. I started working this way with students in secondary school and, over time, meeting with good success there, received requests to work with children in primary and infant schools. On the solution-focused principle of 'if it works, do more of it', I did not change what I was doing, but adapted it while staying true to the original model.

For you as a teacher, if you choose to take up solution-support in your practice, you do not need any additional resources or training in how to use them although it will undoubtedly help you to develop your work as a member of the solution-focused community. Also, solution-support is portable, you can use it wherever you are and do not need a specific meeting space. Space is always at a premium in schools and I often meet students in the corridor, or outside if the weather is fine, always checking to make sure that the school office knows where we are, and that we are in full sight of other teaching staff.

If you look at the recommended titles given in Chapter 10 on the solution-focused approach, you will notice some differences between solution-support and solution-focused brief therapy (SFBT), which is the framework that guides solution-focused support in its most widely applied form. When I started using this approach I followed the SFBT guidelines closely. Over time, while staying true to the model, I slimmed it down to fit the needs of the students and schools more closely. This is a talking approach, and I use the solution-support structure – as I have illustrated it in this chapter – with students from 5 to 18 years of age. While the structure is consistent, obviously the conversation with a very young student will have its own language and style, and be different from that with an older student.

With the youngest students, the overall structure may be simplified to problem-free talk, with the focus on what is going well, the task and scaling. With older students I use the full solution-support structure, and if working with older students and parents, or other adults, I may use the SFBT 'miracle question'. For further explanation, look at the references at the end of this chapter and at the last chapter in this book.

References

Deci, E.L. (1972) 'The effects of contingent and non-contingent rewards and controls on intrinsic motivation', *Organizational Behavior and Human Performance*, 8 (2): 217–29.

Pink, D. H. (2009) *Drive: The Surprising Truth about What Motivates Us*. London: Riverhead.

Taylor, T. (2016, in press) *The Beginner's Guide to Mantle of the Expert*. Publisher: Author.

7

TALKING ABOUT PEDAGOGY

This chapter will give you the opportunity to:

- think about your understanding of pedagogy
- relate your pedagogical understanding to the teaching for behaviour change
- relate your pedagogical knowledge to a story of a student with a complex problem in school

The title of this book is *Transforming Behaviour in the Classroom* and might be expected to focus on management of behaviour. So why have I included this chapter on pedagogy? When you teach you are doing pedagogical work encompassing a range of activities with a matching set of intended outcomes, to do with your students' learning and their behaviour while they are learning. I believe that it is vital to understand what you are doing pedagogically to be able to reflect on what you might do better, in the interest of students' learning and 'behaviour'.

What is pedagogy?

Pedagogy is variously described as the science and art of education, as the theoretical study of how best to teach, as the function of a teacher or the instructional methods used by teachers, though that does not necessarily help to make it clearer. The Swiss educational thinker Pestalozzi in the nineteenth century conceptualized a pedagogy centred on the child, rooted in human nature, connecting to values such as compassion and peace and fully engaging the strengths and resources we each have. Albert Einstein said that his education at the Pestalozzi School at Aarau helped him realize the superiority of education based on free action and personal responsibility, rather than one relying on outward authority. This educational experience is acknowledged as inspiring Einstein's creative approaches to problem solving and his use of theoretical thought experiments in his later research.

The educationalists Steiner, Montessori and Dewey in the twentieth century broadened these pedagogical possibilities, describing education as a social process of living in the moment rather than being primarily a preparation for the future. This is progressive pedagogy, leading students to a place where they can learn for themselves or walking with them along the learning path. From this perspective students use and deepen their strengths and resources to create their own knowledge. Here knowledge means more than information to be delivered: it is also interpretation and performance, which is difficult to communicate and uncertain, and leads on to the realization of a person's full potential. In contrast to these student-centred 'head, heart, hands' pedagogues who aim to engage the whole person, others treat knowledge as data to be delivered by the teacher. An example of a pedagogy taking this perspective is direct instruction, the teaching of a body of knowledge, drilling learning into students to fulfil a predesigned plan. In the UK it underpins primary school literacy and maths teaching and drives the 'back to basics' political purpose of a recent Minister of State for Education. The twentieth-century Brazilian educationist Paulo Freire (1998a, 1998b) called this approach the 'banking' of knowledge. He warned of the danger of treating learners like objects to be manipulated, like the pigeons and rats in the Skinner's experiments. Freire's critical pedagogy emphasizes dialogue over curriculum content, with students in formal and informal settings as people to be related to. He believed that teachers should look out for 'teachable moments' that might lie outside the formal curriculum.

Coming back to the practical teaching of behaviour, pedagogy entered my thinking early on in my own work in a private special school for students diagnosed with emotional and behavioural difficulties. They had been assessed and categorized by educational psychologists who played no further practical role in the education of these children after they had been placed in the school at which I worked. The psychological diagnosis of a student's deficit made a pedagogical requirement to remedy the deficit through teaching, if possible, with the responsibility transferred to me as their teacher. Doing the right thing in my approach to the learning needs of these students might enable them to learn their way over or past the barriers presented by their apparent special needs. What was needed was an appropriate and effective pedagogy for students who had emotional and behavioural needs that affected their learning to such an extent they had been removed from their mainstream schools and their childhood friends and sent off to live miles away in a rural village. Whatever had been offered pedagogically in their previous mainstream schools had not resulted in their inclusion. Was it good enough to repeat what had gone before? What were the alternatives, if any? I knew very little about it when I started teaching, and that is what drove me start exploring.

Divide and conquer

Behaviour and learning have become largely separated as pedagogical issues in schools. Pedagogies for learning are becoming better understood, while admittedly still giving rise to fierce disagreement between teachers committed to different pedagogical schools of thought. At least this shows there are some useful tensions building up to power the dialogue. Across the academic curriculum there is a long-established contest over pedagogy, and which outcomes are most important. In the day-to-day reality of classrooms teachers make pedagogical choices, from direct instruction, rote and repetition all the way through to reflective and imaginative inquiry. Different pedagogies are not mutually exclusive but are intended for different learning purposes, to be deployed where most effective. Pedagogy for behaviour lags far behind learning pedagogy, boxed in by behaviourist psychology, where learning is reduced to conditioning, and reward and punishment become the tools of choice to achieve it.

In my training as a teacher 20 years ago, no serious attention was paid to pedagogy and it seems that little has changed in the UK since. There was no mention of behaviour and what was pedagogically possible there. But finding myself wearing the badge of a teacher in a special school a year after qualifying prompted me to think about what was special about me, whether I had any special knowledge or just accepted that reward and punishment were the only options. Were my students really deficient? Should I be the holder of power and responsibility for their behaviour? This feeling was strengthened in moving to teach in a local education authority (LEA) Pupil Referral Unit (PRU) and a new job advising other teachers about behaviour. My PRU had started out in the 1980s at a Child Guidance Clinic managed by psychiatrists, where children with problems were observed while they smashed up a piano and made cakes, while their parents were interviewed by the psychiatrists about what had gone wrong.

After a few years, educational psychologists took over when the psychiatrists withdrew, then the psychologists left too, to be replaced by teachers with no special training. Responsibility was progressively transferred from mental health specialists to educational psychologists to teachers, and external support was withdrawn. Unlike mainstream schools, which all had an educational psychologist and often a school nurse in attendance, the PRU had no such provision. It was up to us as teachers to develop our pedagogical expertise to fill the gap. A similar withdrawal from mainstream schools is happening with the reduction in child and adolescent mental health services (CAMHS), and in some cases the disappearance of LEA support services. It is up to teachers to take on the support of all students as the bar for referral to specialist services is being raised. So what pedagogical alternatives are available to us, how do we know that we can work safely and ethically with all students, and how do we know when to call for additional support from external specialists?

Case story: Jumping the barriers

A special event

A few years ago I was invited to an Outstanding Achievement Award ceremony for young people in care, organized by a LEA. A colleague who worked as a care coordinator had invited me, telling me that a student, Edward, who I had worked with some time before, would be there. When I arrived, people were chatting in the foyer and I recognized my ex-student, standing with people I assumed were his foster carers. The ceremony got underway and Edward duly went up on to the stage to get his award for Year 7 peer mentoring. A teacher from his school spoke about how he supported new entrants and helped them to settle in. I had not heard much about him since we finished our work together and it was good to know that he had been successful in school.

An ordinary need

Two years before this ceremony a social worker had contacted me about Edward. He had been banned from going into the science department in his school. He had caused damage in the lab and acted unsafely, he had been warned about the consequences and been punished for it but he had not corrected his behaviour, and the head of science had excluded him from the department. This was a big problem for Edward. The school had followed its behaviour policy scrupulously, he had been excluded for fixed terms to no effect. His carers had been told that the school was considering excluding Edward permanently.

Edward had been in his foster placement for a long time with carers who were highly skilled in caring for young children, and both Edward and his carers felt it was time to move on. His social worker had found new carers. The new placement was in a different town and Edward would have to change schools. If he moved placements at the end of summer term, he would have the summer holidays to settle in and he could start in his new school in September.

The new carers worked full-time, and could offer him a place if he was attending school full time. No school place would mean no foster placement. The social worker had met the head teacher of the new school, who said that provided Edward had a good report from his present school he would be welcome to join in September. Everything tied neatly together, provided Edward very quickly started to behave and got a positive recommendation from his present school. It was halfway through the summer term, so there was not much time to sort out the tangle.

Getting started

Edward's science teacher was an experienced classroom manager and for a student to be banned from the science department for safety reasons meant there were some serious problems to deal with. Edward clearly needed to get back into science lessons in order to be able to show that he could behave properly and then work hard to catch up with work he had missed. I sent a message to the to the head of science:

'What would tell you that Edward could be allowed back into science lessons?'

During the following week he called me to say that with two weeks of good reports from all heads of department, he would allow Edward to return to his class and that Edward's science teacher had agreed to this. A few days later I met Edward in school and after the usual introductions we got down to business.

Me: My job is to meet up with school students who've got a bit stuck, to do some useful work together. I do this work with students in a lot of different schools. I've spoken to your social worker, so I know about your situation and that she's talked to you about this meeting and you agreed to meet me. Is that right?

Edward: Yeah, she said you might be able to help me.

Me: OK, we'll meet once a week for four weeks, for about half an hour. OK?

Edward: Yep.

Me: So what might we work on today that could be useful to you?

Edward: I don't know.

Me: Mmm .... I see. But suppose you did know what might be useful, what might it be?

Edward: My behaviour?

Me: How might that be useful to you if we worked on that?

Edward: I suppose ... because unless I get a good report from here my new school won't take me.

Me: Mmm. So if we did some work on your behaviour and you got a good report to take to your new school, how would that be good for you?

Edward: Well, I want to go to my new foster placement so I have to change schools. But they might not take me because of my behaviour.

Me: OK. So is that our project? Something to do with your behaviour?

Edward: Yep.

Me: Let's come back to it later on. I'd like to ask you about something completely different. What's your best thing? What do you like to do best?

Edward: Do you mean in school time or ...?

Me: Any time really.

Edward: Oh right. My best thing is parkour.

I'd never heard of parkour before and I asked him to tell me about it. He said it was about running and jumping across an area and he usually did it with a few other people. He told me it was scary and fun. I asked him if he was any good at it and he said he was. I asked him what made him good at it. He said he had good balance, he was strong, he could make his mind up quickly what to do, he'd decide without stopping to think about it.

Me: So what is it that makes you good at parkour, is it your sense of balance, being strong, being able to make your mind up quickly about what to do? Is that right?

Edward: Yeah ... Because you move fast in places you've never been before so have to decide what to do about your next jump.

Me: OK ... Well, thanks for telling me about parkour. That's new to me. Let's come back to our project about your behaviour. If I asked you to put yourself on a scale of 1–10 for this project, where 1 is for you being out of your science class for doing whatever it was and 10 is for you in your new placement and making a good start in your new school at the beginning of next term, where would you say you are right now?

I sketched the scale line in my notebook and watched as he put a mark on the line at 6.

Me: How come you are at 6 and not at 1?

Edward: Because I'm behaving myself?

Me: What are you doing differently that tells you that you have moved up to 6?

Edward: Not mucking about in classes.

Me: So what are you doing instead of mucking about in class?

Edward: Getting on with my work.

Me: So if I asked your head of science what he's hearing from other teachers about you, that would tell him you should be back in science classes, what would that be?

Edward: That I'm behaving myself.

Me: Which lessons would that be in?

Edward: All of them.

Me: What have you got next?'

Edward: Double art.

Me: If I asked your art teacher what she noticed about you that impressed her, what might she say?

Edward: She'd say I've stopped messing about and I'm getting on with my work.

Me: Right. Let's go back to your scale. Where do you hope you might be on the scale by the end of the art lesson?

He marks the scale at 9.

Me: Mmm ... how would you know? What would tell you that?

Edward: I'd have been getting on with my work, no mucking about for the whole lesson.

Me: How come you'd be able to do that?

Edward: I just can.

Me: We need to finish now. There are two things to do. I'll come in to see you again next week and when we meet I'm going to ask you what you've noticed that tells you things are going well. So that's your job over the next week, to notice things going well. So tell me what's your job?

Edward: Notice things going well.

Me: Exactly. What have you noticed that's gone well over the last half an hour?

Edward: Er ... Talking to you, telling you about parkour?

Me: I agree. That's your job over the next week, to notice what's going well, and I'll ask you about it when we meet next week. The last thing is compliments. Who do you want to go first?

Edward: You.

Me: My compliment to you is about the way you've worked today. I've asked you a lot of questions and you've answered all of them. That's my compliment to you, about your work. What's your compliment to yourself?

Edward: It's about my scale.

Me: So what about that?

Edward: I've said I'll be at 9.

Me: I'll see you next week Edward, and I'll ask you about what you've noticed going well.

Edward: OK. Bye Geoffrey.

I met Edward five times over a month. We quickly settled into a routine which took about 20 minutes each time. He kept on noticing what was going well. We used the scale to track and confirm his progress. He was back in science at the start of the third week. At our last meeting Edward paid me an unprompted compliment on the work I had done. I met his social worker again and she told me Edward's new school place and his new foster placement were both secured. He would be moving at the start of the summer holidays. Two years later I watched Edward as he walked up onto the stage to received his award.

A prize-winning pedagogy

Edward had changed his behaviour quickly; during the course of a 30-minute conversation he had identified what he had to do in order for his best hopes to be realised. He had made an assessment of where he was in relation to his best hope, and the rate of change that it was necessary to achieve. Back in class he started doing what was necessary and kept it up consistently.

The evidence of change was in his achievement. My role as a teacher can be seen in the story as it emerges. I had to become familiar with the context of Edward's problem, but taking the solution-focused approach meant I investigated what Edward's world would be like with the problem solved, rather than looking into the problem itself. I was not interested in problem details, such as what happened in the science laboratory and how, when or why it had happened. I did not look for what might have caused his behaviour, what behaviour analysts call 'triggers'. In the meeting with Edward, I facilitated his reflective inquiry into his best hope for the outcome of the project, his competencies and strengths and his current position with the project. I asked him to notice his successes in the moment and gave him a learning task to look out for signs of success, for flashes of flow. Edward carried out his task, tracked his own progress, independently adjusted his behaviour in school at an appropriate rate of change and achieved his best hope within the allocated time.

REFLECTION

Placing Edward as the student and myself as the teacher, can we say this is pedagogical work?
    If so, what kind of pedagogy were we engaged in?

Pedagogical questions and making pedagogical choices

Before I entered the story, Edward's teachers had been responsible for teaching him to behave in school. Of course, students are influenced by people other than their teachers, but schools have an identified responsibility for students' learning across a curriculum that extends beyond the academic subjects. An aspect of this is the personal, health and social education curriculum (PHSE), non-statutory in the 2014 National Curriculum in England (DfE, 2014), which means there is no official programme of study to be followed. However, schools are told by the Department of Education that they 'should make provision for PSHE education, drawing on good practice'. Presumably 'good practice' would include telling students the rules and routines of school and the punishments laid down in behaviour policy for infringement of what are intended to be aids to learning.

An example of a programme of study is offered by the UK PSHE Association on its website. I am referring to it without implying a recommendation. Here PSHE is presented as an important component of the broad school curriculum covering a wide spectrum of learning. It includes personal development; building of confidence, resilience and self-esteem; risk management and decision making; the building and shaping of the individual student's identity; understanding and accommodating difference and change; understanding emotions; social communication (PSHE Association, 2014). And the intended learning outcomes? Students' self-knowledge, empathy and team working skills, work skills for employability and for the better enjoyment and management of their lives. And 'behaviour'. If PSHE had been successful for Edward, maybe we would never had met.

How is this suggested PSHE curriculum to be taught? A programme of study divided into topics or themes is taught through the pedagogy of thematic instruction. Thematic instruction relates cognitive skills such as reading, memorizing and writing to the context of daily life. It shifts the focus of learning away from subject areas and towards issues. As a thematic instructor, you would decide which PSHE topics to work on, how long to spend on each one, and start looking for materials. From the available materials you can select the specific areas of knowledge within a topic to teach. Because this method is issue-based, individual topics are indeterminate; so, for example, what knowledge should be taught in order for students to be able to manage risk would be a matter for the teacher to decide. The real-life situations chosen to teach risk management and the function of the new learning would depend largely on the materials and experiences the teacher has been able to assemble, with very little consistency. Was thematic instruction going to be the pedagogical aid for Edward as he rushed towards the school exit door? We had to do something different to get a quick win. But what?

Behaviour policy, pedagogy and practice

All schools in the UK are supposed to have a learning policy and a behaviour policy. School inspectors expect to see them when they visit. Edward's school had a typical secondary school behaviour policy effectively laying out the school's behaviour curriculum. It opened positively, saying that the school supported the personal, social and moral development of all students and nurtured self-discipline, respect for self and others and the environment, the ability to question and argue rationally and habits of responsibility and self-discipline. It said that all students were treated as being sensible and responsible. It laid out in detail what represented good behaviour. It stated that the behaviour policy was not punitive, but it had a whole page listing 'sanctions' and an appendix on 'punishment' to be applied to students who break the rules. Pupils were to have the code of conduct printed in their school planners.

How did the school intend to teach the behaviour curriculum as described in the behaviour policy? To a behavioural psychologist, learning means the acquiring of new behaviours, in response to external stimuli. Punishments are set out in a behaviour policy document as external stimuli to promote learning in those students who do not know the rules, or still break them if they do. The most popular approach to teaching based on behavioural psychology is known as 'direct instruction'. A number of features of this approach suggest that, at least superficially, it is the pedagogy intended for the delivery of the behaviour curriculum. For example, a core principle of direct instruction is that the teacher is responsible for student learning. If students fail to learn it is because the teacher has failed to teach. As the Ofsted Chief Inspector has put it, the excellent teacher exudes authority in the classroom, controlling and directing the learning and behaviour of the students in the room (Ofsted, 2013).

The full method of direct instruction utilizes instructional scripts, drilling, practice and systematic correction of errors as pre-planned steps. The curriculum, not the student-as-person, is the focus and such learning outcomes as improved self-esteem and getting on with self and others are de-emphasized. For teaching behaviour, psychological behaviourism and its educational partner, pedagogical direct instruction, have become the default pedagogy. With this method, a student is conditioned to behave according to the school rules using the behaviourist regime of punishment and reward as reinforcers of learning. The intention is that if the student fails to comply, increasing severity of punishment will support this new learning. The behaviourist perspective on the learner, that 'it's the behaviour not the child' as the target for conditioning, is intentionally depersonalizing and dehumanizing. Isolation from other students, removal from social times in school, school detention in school time and at weekends, and fixed-term and permanent exclusion are accepted as suitable punishments for use in the operant conditioning programme for rule-breakers.

As Sir Michael Wilshaw, the current Chief Inspector of schools and head of Ofsted put it, 'It isn't rocket science. Children need to know the rules and teachers need to know they will be supported in enforcing them,' adding that leaders of the best schools are successful in explaining and enforcing their expectations to staff, pupils and parents. He said, 'I see too many schools where head teachers are blurring the lines between friendliness and familiarity – and losing respect along the way. After all, every hour spent with a disruptive, attention-seeking pupil is an hour away from ensuring other pupils are getting a decent education' (*Guardian*, 2014). Direct instruction and punitive enforcement fit together, depersonalized conditioning that eliminates the danger of blurring the lines of authority. This approach may work for the large majority of already compliant students, because they do as they are told. But what happens when it does not work? What about Edward? He had experienced direct instruction and conditioning by reward and punishment. He needed something different and he was running out of time. What made the difference was making the shift from problem-focused to solution-focused thinking and solution-support.

Doing something different

From time to time in the early 2000s my employers provided a compulsory whole-service training day entitled 'An introduction to solution-focused brief therapy'. I worked in a school in the morning and turned up at midday, had a lovely lunch served by members of the local Women's Institute, and then we started the afternoon session. It was presented by Harvey Ratner, one of the owners of BRIEF (www.brief.org.uk), who introduced the solution-focused approach to the UK.

Harvey presented the key ideas at the heart of solution-focused brief therapy, and asked us as a group if we could frame some questions we might ask a client based on these principles. I thought it seemed easy and put my hand up. I asked my question and Harvey gently suggested that while my question was useful, there might be a better way to put it. He rephrased it as a solution-focused question and offered it back to me. I realized it was not that easy, and at the end of a fascinating session I asked him how I could find out more about the approach.

At about the same time I had received a referral asking for behaviour support for a boy in his last year at primary school. The referral said that he was at the highest risk of permanent exclusion because of his violence to other children in his school. He was known to the police. The referral suggested that a significant factor may have been that he had witnessed a very violent act on a family friend when he was much younger, and had never received any counselling or support to deal with this.

The referral asked for an immediate response from me, as the school had tried everything they could and were close to permanently excluding him, despite their sympathy for him and his family. I was worried that if I entered this potentially traumatic situation I could make things worse, as I did not know how to guarantee his safety whilst trying to so something useful. The usual behaviour support approach would have been to ask him about what had gone wrong and try to find out what was the real problem. I was not prepared to get into that.

The difference that made the difference

With the introductory training and reading *Solutions in Schools* (Ajmal and Rees, 2001) I knew that the solution-focused approach gave me a way forward. The referral inferred that the trauma the student had experienced might be causing his violent behaviour, but of course it might not be true.

I was a teacher, not a therapist, and I had no professional remit to get involved in this question. If I were to take the solution-focused approach, at best we could make progress and, importantly, at worst I could do no harm.

I made a start, *Solutions in Schools* in one hand, pen in the other, the young student and his mum in front of me. My first solution-focused session. He stopped fighting and played more football. We did a lot of talking about what he was good at. He never mentioned the terrible event from his childhood. He made a successful transfer to secondary school and stayed there.

Conclusion

Five years later I walked up the steps into the theatre and the award ceremony. In between I had responded to many requests for help in often seemingly hopeless situations. I knew I could rely on solution-support, every time in every situation.

How does it work?

What is the difference that makes the difference?

These questions take us into the next chapter.

References

Ajmal, Y. and Rees, I. (2001) *Solutions in Schools: Creative Applications of Solution Focused Brief Thinking with Young People and Adults.* London: BT Press.

Department for Education (DfE) (2014) *The National Curriculum in England.* London: DfE.

Freire, P. (1998a) *Pedagogy of Hope.* New York: Continuum.

Freire, P. (1998b) *Pedagogy of the Oppressed*, New Revised 20th-Anniversary edn. New York: Continuum.

Guardian (2014) 'Headteachers too soft on unruly pupils, says Ofsted chief Sir Michael Wilshaw'. Available at: www.theguardian.com/education/2014/sep/25/headteachers-too-soft-unruly-pupils-ofsted-chief-sir-michael-wilshaw (accessed 11 May 2015).

Ofsted (2013) 'Ofsted Annual Report 2012/13: Schools report'. Available at: www.gov.uk/government/publications/ofsted-annual-report-201213-schools-report (accessed 11 May 2015).

PSHE Association (2014) 'PSHE education programme of study (key stages 1 – 4)'. Available at: www.pshe-association.org.uk/resources_search_details.aspx?ResourceId=495 (accessed 11 May 2015).

8

MOTIVATION AND CHANGING BEHAVIOUR

This chapter will give you the opportunity to:

- think about how change is motivated
- consider how you can support student motivation to change behaviour

Praise, reward and punishment as motivators of change

Advice on becoming an effective teacher routinely highlights the importance of building a relationship with students and focusing on engagement. An effective teacher gets these right and students will be motivated to cooperate and to learn.

A 15-year-old student in a mainstream school was falling far behind his teachers' expectations for his exam grades. Subject teachers, pastoral and senior staff had tried all the usual means to get him to catch up, to complete his coursework and to take more interest in what he was doing. They were frustrated that he had considerable potential that seemed to be going to waste. He was clearly not motivated to work.

A senior teacher made a referral to my service for support. She told me that she knew I had worked with students in the school who had behaviour problems and wondered if there was anything I could possibly do with this student, who was not exactly a behaviour case but seemed to be stuck and to have given up trying. The school had used their behaviour policy systematically, but the student had not changed and he was seriously underachieving. I arranged to meet him, no big committee, just the two of us. I asked the senior teacher if she would let him know that he might find the meeting useful in getting a clearer understanding of what he was hoping for in the last few months of school and afterwards. I was told that the parents were very keen to try anything that might help their son.

No show

I went into school as arranged. I was shown to the meeting room by my contact in school, who went to collect the student. She came back after a while to tell me he was not coming to meet me. It had taken her a while because he was out on the playing field. She apologized, but I reassured her that it was not her responsibility. Missed meetings happened and I was always prepared for that. I asked her to let the student know that I would be in school, same time, same place next week. I looked forward to meeting him then and asked her to remind him of the work we might do together, to help him get clear about what he was hoping for in school and after he left. The next week he was waiting for me in the meeting room when I arrived. I apologized for being a few minutes late. We exchanged names and I asked him if he had any idea what the meeting was about. He said he had been told it was about where he was hoping to get to.

> *Me:* So is that a good enough reason for us to be meeting today? To do some work on where you are hoping to get to?
>
> *Student:* Yes.
>
> *Me:* Good. Let's put that to one side for a while. I'd like to ask you about something different.

You will be getting to know what comes next by now, if you have read other chapters with stories of solution-focused teaching.

I asked him what he liked doing best, what he was good at, what other people thought he was good at, what his teachers noticed he was going well and what strengths they recognized in him. I asked him what it was about him that impressed his class mates. As he talked I made brief notes.

After about 10 minutes I checked back with him on what I had noted down, his strengths and resources, and asked him if they were true about him. He said he thought they were.

> *Me:* Now let's get back to the project and question we put to one side; about where you're hoping to get to. You finish here next summer and I wonder what is your best hope for the rest of time you have in school?

He said he hoped to do well in his exams and to go to college to do his A-levels after he left school. I drew a 1–10 scale in my notebook and handed him the book and my pen.

Me: If 10 is where you'll be after the end of summer term, your exams have gone well and you're starting the long holiday knowing you've done OK ... 1 is where you were exactly a week ago .... Where would you put yourself on the scale right now?

He marked it at 7.

Me: Seven tells me that you're already doing a lot to get to 10 by the end of term. What tells you you're at 7?

Student: I've done a lot of my course work over the last week.

Me: I see. What would your teachers be noticing that would tell them you're at 7?

Student: I've stopped messing about and I'm just getting the work done.

Me: I see. So how come you've been able to do that? What is it about you that you can stop messing about and get the work done?

Student: I suppose I know I can do OK if I do a bit more work. I want to get a good job.

Me: Where do you hope you might be on the scale, say in a week's time?

Student: Eight?

Me: I see. We need to finish now, we've got two minutes left. Two things to do, to offer you a compliment and ask you to do a job. Your job is to notice what's going well for you. Would it be useful to you to meet again next week?

Student: Yes.

Me: Then when we meet next week I'll ask you about what you've noticed going well. My compliment to you is about working independently, about making up your mind to sort things out in school and getting with it over the last week. That's what I noticed when you marked the scale at 7. Now will you give yourself a compliment?

Student: OK. It's about the same thing, that I know what to do and I've just got on with it.

The next time we met for 10 minutes. He told me what was going well, he marked the scale at 8 and said he knew what he had to do to get to 10. I asked him if it would be useful to meet again and he said he thought we didn't need to. He said he knew what he should be doing, he just had not done it until now.

I complimented him and gave him the same task to keep on looking for what was going well and we said goodbye. I went towards the staffroom to meet the teacher who had made the referral to let her know the student and I had finished our work and things seemed to be going well.

> *Teacher*: 'It's amazing. How does whatever you do work so fast? You've only met him twice.
>
> *Me*: Because I'm not the one doing the work. The student is doing it and he is working on it all the time. It's the solution-focused way of doing the job and that's what happens.

REFLECTION

How come the student made the significant change in the week before we had our first meeting? I had sent him a message, that we might do some work on his best hope for school and he just got on with it on his own.

- What is the nature of his motivation to solve the problem here?
- What can you say about our relationship?

The question of motivation

It was not that this student had no motivation to succeed. He came to school every day in his school uniform, he sat in class, he did not cause any trouble in class, he enjoyed being with his friends, he did all that for his own reasons. But as all teenagers should do at their time in life, he made choices and exercised his independence in some areas. He chose not to do coursework, he chose not to come to meet me and he chose to make a start on sorting things out on his own. Then he chose to meet me and chose not to finish when the work was done. We had not talked about the problem, other than using it to name our project. I had given him no advice or guidance. I complimented him but did not praise him for his achievement. I had not asked him how he felt about what he was doing. I focused on action, on what was happening and the evidence of change. As it turned out, he carried the project through on his own. By the time we did meet he was already well on his way with his own solution to his problem.

In the course of your training you will have come across a range of pedagogical options across the broad curriculum, which you have been able to see in action, or put into practice for yourself. There are some very different pedagogies available for our use as teachers, covering a spectrum from fully teacher-centred to fully student-centred and each has its own associated type of implied or stated relationship between teacher and student.

REFLECTION

Think through the type of relationship between teacher and student that forms the basis of 1) teacher-centred pedagogy and 2) student-centred pedagogy, in terms of control, responsibility, agency and motivation.
    Make some notes of this in your journal.

From the pragmatic point of view, the pedagogy we adopt depends on what we are teaching. The pedagogy of inquiry that I am illustrating with stories from my practice works, and it helps me to be an effective teacher. Taking a pragmatic view, a 'practice-to-theory' approach enables me to skirt around the traditional/progressive contest that some educators engage in. It also frees up some space to think about the moral and ethical implications of our practical work as teachers.

Doing more of what works and not taking sides

When we are hoping to change disruptive behaviour of some students, they are commonly seen to be unmotivated to make a change. You can have rock-steady control and punishment and it does not seem to make a difference, although it might physically remove the problem. You can have a bedrock of non-judgemental care and concern and that does not necessarily draw them towards changing their ways either. Some teachers and educational writers insist that there is a stark pedagogical choice to be made between teacher-centred control and discipline or student-centred mayhem in the classroom, justifying the need for compliance as a starting point for effec- tive teaching. This either/or choice is commonly wrapped up in the language of traditional versus progressive education, characterizing the alternatives as disciplined and managed or the teacher abdicating their responsibilities. More thoughtfully, others say that if there was something other than reward and punishment, particularly an alternative to punishment as a routine approach to disruptive behaviour, they would take it but there does not seem to be a reliable and practicable alternative. What these teachers are hoping for is cooperative, independently minded students, who can challenge and be challenged within safe, clear boundaries. A great deal of evidence points to the failure of the control and external discipline approach in achieving this (Webs of Substance, 2013). There is general agreement in the literature on the features of a pedagogy that promotes learning and prevents low-level behaviour problems. The features include engagement, relevance, purpose, participation, student self-evaluation, pace and positive feedback.

What does it mean to be an effective teacher?

There is general agreement about what it means to be an effective teacher, backed up a by a wealth of evidence from research spanning the pedagogical spectrum from highly teacher-centred to highly student-centred teaching. At one end of the spectrum is teacher-centred direct instruction. This has been promoted by Hattie (2009), who carried out a large-scale meta-analysis of 800 published research studies on effectiveness. The findings demonstrated the effectiveness of this approach for teaching specific skills, and it is widely used in teaching literacy, numeracy and mathematics skills in schools in the UK and the US. As an instructor fully in control of the class and the subject matter, the teacher decides the learning intentions and success criteria, makes them transparent to the students, demonstrates them by modelling, evaluates students' understanding of what they have been told, and re-tells them by tying it all together with the learning intentions made clear at the start (2009: 49). As what might be seen as a footnote to this process of teacher-centred instruction in a highly structured environment, Rozzelle and Gregory (2010) add that the process begins with setting the stage for learning and there is a gradual release of responsibility from the teacher to the students in the course of the programme.

Effective direct instructors are described as mindful teachers who can spot potential behaviour problems and take preventative action while maintaining emotional objectivity. They promote classroom cohesiveness by creating a sense that the classroom community is working together towards positive learning gains (Hattie, 2009: 102–103). They promote positive teacher–student relationships by respecting and building upon what each student brings to the classroom through listening, empathy and having a positive regard for others (2009: 118). This makes sense, because even given the most highly planned structure there are students in the room who do not necessarily fit into it. They have to be engaged. Talking about effective visible learning teachers Hattie (2009), far from presenting the teacher as the programmer of students as automatons, says that to be effective teachers need to be mindful, emotionally mature and empathetic, actively listening and having positive regard for their students. The effective teacher deploying the direct instruction pedagogy shows caring and respect for students' needs, responses and diversity.

In a more recent book on visible learning, Hattie and Yates (2013) discuss the positive impact of good teacher–student relationships. They cite research evidence confirming that friendly and warm conditions in class improve students' test performance and establish long-term persistent gains in their attainment and attitude to school. However, in the teacher-centred classroom, given the friendly and warm conditions established in the room and the need for preventative action when the teacher spots potential behaviour problems, Hattie and Yates (2013) do not offer an alternative to established punitive strategies for correcting unwanted behaviour.

REFLECTION

How could solution-support be used in a teacher-centred classroom to address behaviour problems?

What, if any, features of the direct-instruction approach match those of solution-focused teaching, in terms of the motivation of students to learn? You might think back to the story above to help you with this.

Moving to the opposite end of the pedagogical spectrum, what would an effective student-centred teacher be doing, compared to an effective teacher-centred one? The Montessori method is a well-known example of student-centred education, developed by Maria Montessori a century ago and found in about 20,000 schools worldwide. The effective Montessori teacher first creates a calm and joyful atmosphere in an environment that allows each child to connect to productive work. The teacher engages students with a full complement of specially designed Montessori learning materials, meticulously arranged and available for use in an aesthetically pleasing environment. The classroom is prepared by the teacher to encourage independence, freedom within limits and a sense of order. In other words, thought-out classroom management.

The pedagogical strategies are very different in the positioning of the teacher in holding or sharing control over the factual knowledge content part of the curriculum, but in terms of the intended relationship between teacher and student Hattie and Yates' (2013) 'friendly and warm conditions' closely match up with Montessori's 'calm and joyful atmosphere'. Montessori uses a model of teacher–environment–student, creating a learning triangle. Hattie and Yates (2013) do the same, albeit in a different language, with the same intention for students to grow as well-informed and independently acting people. The importance of this relationship is well-known to established teachers, and is referred to by educational experts as a vital factor in establishing a cooperative and resilient working environment in the classroom. As you enter teaching it is likely that you are already fully aware of its importance. The question is, how do you make it happen?

The hard edge of changing behaviour

In this book I have offered you evidence, in the form of stories, from my own practice over two decades. My best hope is that you will begin to feel more confident in building your own practice as an autonomous professional, based on evidence that rings true to you. These stories have been about students making changes and becoming more successful in school. I applied the solution-focused approach in as many settings as I could, given that I was in full-time work and without access to any research funding. I was not on my own. A team developed of five solution-focused teachers: Martin Bohn, Jill Brooks, Anna James, Gill King and me. Between us we have trained, taught, supervised and supported hundreds of individuals in many different learning and work settings. We have met regularly to review our work, to supervise one another and to develop our thinking, and still do so in different circumstances. We found that being solution-focused was always useful to those we worked with and to ourselves, and over time it has become our default way of thinking and our routine approach to changing behaviour in schools. We also work within a large international community of solution-focused workers who find the approach useful in promoting change. We are convinced and advocate the use of an approach which does not use praise, reward and punishment as the means of changing behaviour and does not attempt to understand the cause of a problem in order to try to change it through reward or punishment.

Reward and punishment as motivators for change are assumed to be the best approach we have in schools, to the point of being the only approach we have. What is the evidence to support their use? The general argument is that while it is accepted that with the most difficult students punishment does not work reliably in the long term, nothing else has been shown to work any better. There is also the issue of natural justice, that students who have done wrong should not be allowed to get away with it and a sharp dose of punishment corrects the imbalance. The first point is true, that the worst students or people in general do not change their ways, even when they are severely punished. Punishment does not make them better and when punishment means discipline then it comes under question. Kohn, a teacher, investigated this in his book *Punished by Rewards* (1999), which advocated no external discipline. His contemporary Coloroso (in Charles, 1999 p.217) agreed with Kohn that students have a great capacity to regulate their own behaviour in class, but argued for a middle position on discipline where events happen naturally in the real world (e.g. like peers giving negative feedback to an uncooperative team member and the latter apologizing to the group for not doing their job). Thinking through what constitutes a natural consequence in Coloroso's (Charles, 1999) terms and establishing this in class is a reasonable approach for a beginning teacher. But regulating behaviour in a thoughtful way does not necessarily mean using punishment.

What has happened since Kohn's 'Punished by Reward'?

Since Kohn's (1999) book, evidence has been accumulating from many fields of activity that punishment and reward do not change bad behaviour into good behaviour, but behaviourism has largely maintained its grip on behaviour in schools. It cannot be through lack of evidence but that may be because no practical and theoretical alternative has been offered, at least until the solution-focused approach became available, and sufficiently well known that teachers felt they could take the risk and try it out.

It has become increasingly clear that punishment and reward do not motivate students to change. In fact the reverse is true. Kohn (1999) quoted evidence that students with highly controlling teachers had lower self-esteem and lower intrinsic self-motivation in attempting to make changes than those with teachers who supported them in making choices. If we believe that motivation is something that people do rather than something that gets done to them, then this is significant. Nearly 20 years later, Pink (2009) wrote about the paradox of a practice being sustained in the face of good evidence, showing that it is at least ineffective and at worst harmful. He refers back to Kohn (1999) on motivation and reward and to Dweck (2006) on the significance of mindset. Research quoted by Pink (2009) provides evidence that using external motivators with a complex creative task has uncertain outcomes including:

• extinguishing intrinsic motivation
• diminishing performance and creativity
• inhibiting good behaviour and encouraging cheating, shortcuts and unethical behaviour
• performance only for the reward itself
• short-term thinking.

Given that praise, reward and punishment are the usual tools of choice in schools for changing behaviour despite the drawbacks, how do you make an informed decision about what to do when you go about changing behaviour? Pink (2009) addressed this in pointing out 'the narrow band of circumstances in which carrots and sticks do their job reasonably well'.

In some circumstances it is difficult to make the connections that bring routine tasks to life, such as following the daily procedure for registration in school. It just has to be done and an external motivator such as commenting to the class that registration has gone well every day for the last two weeks and they will get a class award cannot undermine students' sense of autonomy and their intrinsic motivation that goes with it, because it is not their choice, it is just a set procedure with little intrinsic motivation involved. Reward may improve performance in a routine task with little associated risk. But if the task invited more creativity and relied more on intrinsic motivation (e.g. if the students decided to tidy their base room at the end of each day and organized their own rota for doing it), an extrinsic reward would lead to poorer performance of the task. Fully relevant to our thinking here, if a student were making self-motivated changes in their behaviour through their own efforts in the course of solution-support, it is essential to eliminate the use of praise–reward–punishment external motivation because this will collapse their sense of autonomy, mastery and purpose with regard to the task. When we as teachers jump from our reliance on external to internal motivation and back again with no warning, students find it confusing. Are we expecting them to be short-term or long-term thinkers? Are they supposed to be autonomous or do they have to follow a rule? It is confusing for me to do it, and it is likely the same for them.

Conclusion

In this chapter I have asked you to reflect on the question of student's motivation to change their behaviour. I have challenged the assumption that reward and punishment are the best tools we have as teachers to promote behaviour change. As a beginning teacher this is the world you are entering, and you have to chart a course between potential and performance, what you must do and what you might do in your practice. As a teacher you might be looking at this theoretical work and be asking, how do I choose which way to go and what effect will it have on my students? What can I do practically?

Here is a suggestion. To link classroom tasks with the appropriate motivator, list the tasks that you are going to do to organize your classroom and assign each one to either the 'routine' or the 'creative thinking' category.

External motivators can be linked to changes in the 'routine' category. Change in the 'creative thinking' category would be internally motivated. The 'routine' category will include the non-negotiable, rule-based procedures that you intend to become automatic in your classroom. Rate the performance of each task listed as 'good enough' or 'needs to change'.

Make a new list of the 'needs to change' tasks and ask yourself, 'Suppose one of these were to change and the change would significantly improve the way the class operates, which would have the biggest effect?' Select this as the target for change and decide on the reward you will provide when the goal is reached.

Pink (2009) suggested three practices to supplement rewards, plus one additional consideration:

1. Discuss with students why this task is necessary – for example: so we can spend our time doing more interesting things than coming in and sitting down, and it helps us work as a team.
2. If it is a necessary routine procedure, call it by its name when you talk about it and set it up with students.
3. Allow students to do the task in their own way once you have made the intended outcome clear – for example: settled and ready to start within 2 minutes of coming into the room, so we can get on with the interesting work that is waiting for you – without specifying precisely the way to get there.
4. And keep in mind the elements of self-motivated action: autonomy, mastery, purpose.

Do the same for the tasks in the 'creative thinking' category. Keep in mind the elements of self-motivated action. Identify the task that would be most worth spending time on. Discuss it with the students, why it is necessary, and decide how you will all make it work as a classroom team and how you will be able to recognize it working. When it does, come together again as a team to recognize the achievement.

References

Charles, C. (1999) *Building Classroom Discipline*, 6th edn. New York: Addison Wesley Longman.

Dweck, C. S. (2006) *Mindset: The New Psychology of Success*. New York: Random House.

Hattie, J. (2009) *Visible Learning: A Synthesis of Over 800 Meta-Analyses Relating to Achievement*. Abingdon: Routledge.

Hattie, J. and Yates, G. (2013) *Visible Learning and the Science of How We Learn*. Abingdon: Routledge.

Kohn, A. (1999) *Punished by Rewards: The Trouble with Gold Stars, Incentive Plans, A's, Praise, and Other Bribes*. Boston, MA: Houghton Mifflin.

Pink, D. H. (2009) *Drive: The Surprising Truth about What Motivates Us*. London: Riverhead.

Rozzelle, J. and Gregory, V. (2010) 'Visible strategies for increased learning'. Available at: http://education.wm.edu/centers/sli/DLST/links/VTALL/pdf/Visible%20Teaching.pdf (accessed 1 March 2015).

Webs of Substance (2013) 'Visible learning and the science of how we learn: a review'. Available at: https://websofsubstance.wordpress.com/2013/10/21/visible-learning-and-the-science-of-how-we-learn-a-review/ (accessed 1 March 2015).

9

CHANGING HABITS AND CHANGING THINKING

This chapter will give you the opportunity to:

- think about what might be going on in the inside when you take a particular approach to a student's changing behaviour

- develop an argument to support your work as a teacher in changing behaviour

- engage in the process of professional development which will lead to your confident practice with students experiencing change

Understanding rapid change

A consistent feature of the work I have been doing is the rapidity of the change in students' behaviour. As illustrated by the case stories I have included in this book, in many cases a single conversation has resulted in a student behaving in a way that gets them moving in the direction of their best hope, to be in school and be successful. The student hoping for change may need more support after this first meeting, but the change starts very soon, in the first meeting and sometimes even before it has started.

Pink's (2009) third drive, intrinsic motivation, is a possible explanation of what energizes the change, why it happens, but there is something else to think about how it comes about. From the outside, the outcome of solution-support looks like a switch being operated, changing behaviour from one state to another, from one type of behaviour to another. I have been asked by school staff, and parents and carers of students I have worked with, 'How do you do that, how did it happen so fast?' As I was walking to my car after the completion of successful work in an infant school with a young student, his mother caught up with me. 'I just wanted to tell you, I've been talking to my friend about you and what you do. We call you "the child whisperer". You don't seem to be doing anything, and then everything changes.' In a primary school, as another project ended and I was leaving the school, the head teacher said, 'See you again when we need another miracle, then?' It might sometimes seem like magic, but this switching into another way of being is evidence of a real change, and I wanted to try to understand it.

Neuroplasticity: changing brains

What has the concept of brain plasticity got to do with behaviour and behaviour management? Over time occasional occurrences of misbehaviour strengthen into habitual behaviour, to a point where the student appears to be controlled by their habits, which resist, or at least are unchanged by, the standard behaviour management procedures in school. This rapid change away from habitual, unwanted behaviour does not look like conventional learning, with a structured programme of instruction and intended learning outcomes decided by the teacher. To bring about new behaviour through teaching, conventional wisdom was that I should set up the learning goals aimed at cancelling a behaviour habit, specify the steps in the student's learning, provide opportunities for practice, correct errors, and keep the student on target and working hard by judicious use of reward and punishment. With this approach, learning to behave differently, changing behaviour, usually takes time and effort, if it happens at all. But in using the solution-focused approach I noticed that the new learning led to the unwanted habits being switched off and the more successful way of behaving being switched on. How can that happen? It relies on the concept of brain plasticity in action, promoting an alternative neural map, already in existence but dormant, with solution-support providing the teaching framework to enable it.

Brain – hardwired or plastic?

Recently neuroscientists have begun to see the possibly that the brain is plastic and dynamic rather than fixed and unchanging, as had been previously assumed (Merzenich, 2013). They found that one brain area could stand in for another, and this could happen at any time in life. They also discovered that within the brain changes are happening all the time, influenced by internal and external events in the form of information. This contrasts with the earlier conception of the brain having particular areas carrying out specific functions: this is known as 'brain localization theory'. This nineteenth-century thinking, stimulated by Broca and Wernicke in the 1860s, laid the foundations for the mechanical, hardwired model of the brain that still exerts a powerful influence. In Hungary in 1952, András Petö put the idea of brain plasticity into effect for children who had difficulty in controlling their movements, using an educational model in place of the then more usual medical one. He approached the problem with a much wider view of learning together, establishing the concept of conductive education, rather than seeing the process as therapy and cure. This resonates with the development of the solution-focused approach in the 1980s as an educational rather than a medical approach to behaviour change.

Brain plasticity as a phenomenon is now under careful scrutiny. We know that information from the outside environment does affect and refine specific pathways in the brain and that indeed 'you are what you think'. Thinking brings about physical changes in the brain, and to paraphrase Dweck (2006), if you think you can achieve something, or think you cannot, you are right. Neuroscientists are working towards the scientific explanation of brain plasticity, how plasticity works at a cellular level and how the world outside and inside environment of the body interact in the development of three-dimensional 'cortical maps'. They are also interested in the degree of plasticity the brain retains throughout life. From this perspective the brain is not seen as a type of computer, made up of fixed components, responding to programming. The brain, or rather the brain and mind, is conscious and responding moment by moment to all kinds of stimuli, including thoughts and emotions. In the process it changes and it produces actions as thoughts and emotions, behaviour and movement. The idea of brain plasticity is entering public awareness on a broad front and is a useful explanatory concept in thinking about what happens when students change their behaviour so abruptly.

Plastic change

One key idea in neuroscientific thinking is that neurones (electrically excitable nerve cells that make up our nervous systems) that fire together, wire together. Brain neurones respond to incoming information and work together in a three-dimensional net to handle it. New information stimulates communication between neurones that may not have worked together before, and the tendency is for them to cooperate to establish a new functional net if the same information is received again. Being familiar, it is assigned to the new net and the relationships between the neurones forming the net strengthen. If the same input is repeated frequently, the net will be repeatedly activated. The connections across the net will become more likely to work together, until the net becomes the most likely destination for that specific information and provide an automatic response. The information is recognized as it enters the brain and is directed towards the destination neural net that demands the least amount of energy to process it.

The plastic brain puts most incoming information into established nets, and makes new connections to attach novel but related information to established nets. Forming habitual nets is a core activity of the plastic brain, and you can understand it from the biological perspective of fitness for survival and the individual's ability to cope with challenges. Seeing a falling rock high above your head and running could be a better survival strategy than standing still and thinking about what to do with the information. The brain continuously scans the environment for information from the outside, where sights, sounds and smells exist, and inside where all kinds of information on hormone levels, temperature, pressure, orientation and so on is routed to the brain. The flow of information to the brain is huge and incessant and the operation of the brain is optimized by incoming information, only being queried if there is something sufficiently novel in it to require the brain to pay attention to it, in order to decide where it should be sent. Despite most incoming information being handled by established neural nets, a great deal of capacity is taken up in running these nets. Only a limited amount of incoming information can be queried at one time and attention paid to it. If there is too much information the overload is effectively ignored (Doidge, 2007).

Neuroscientists using brain imaging have found that new automatic neural nets may take many months to become established, following persistent concentrated effort. Very limited neural nets handling specific, isolated information can establish in the medium term, given sufficient information input by rote learning and practice. In contrast, existing but inactive neural nets rapidly become reactivated in response to key information (Pascual-Leone et al., 2005). This finding that an existing neural net, or habit, can rapidly reactivate given the correct information could explain the rapid change in behaviour we have seen as an outcome of solution-support. The effect of exception-finding in solution-focused work is to engage with information handed by an existing and inactive net. The effect of experiencing flow as information about peak achievement and the open task of looking for more activating information, for what is going well, could relate to the hoped-for change materializing. If your best hope is automaticity in a student's adaptive response to your classroom management and teaching, then activating an existing inactive net which produces that action is a good option. If you accept that the plastic brain is in a constant state of change, the opportunity is always there to develop this capacity for activation, and supports the use of solution-support for changing behaviour.

Cognition

In earlier chapters I have emphasized the influence of behaviourist psychology in providing the current approach to behaviour in many schools. I have also emphasized that the work I have been doing as a teacher I consider to be pedagogical work, not psychological therapy. In raising questions about psychology and its influence in school and schooling, I am not denying the importance and usefulness of the work of psychologists in the field of education. I am interested in finding ways of working that are most advantageous to students and their teachers. There is more to psychology than behaviourism, and another influential school of psychological thought is contributing to making progress with behaviour in schools. Cognitive psychology appeared as a new field of study in the 1960s (Neisser, 1967). Cognitive psychologists investigate how people perceive, remember, think, speak and solve problems. Soon after Neisser's field-defining 1967 book *Cognitive Psychology* appeared, the psychiatrist Aaron Beck developed cognitive behaviour therapy (CBT), a theoretical combination of behaviourism and cognitivism. The behaviourist part involves exposing a person to the thing they fear and avoid, in the hope they will get used to it. The cognitive part challenges errors and distortions in thinking and points out alternatives. Beck proposed that distorted thinking always had a negative effect on behaviour, no matter what type of disorder the person had, and therefore CBT could help in all cases. Beck said his approach was educational, the disordered person being taught that their thinking was distorted, that their core beliefs which they felt were true were in fact wrong, and how to challenge their effects. He characterized the person as failing and disordered and set about trying to correct the deficits. Beck stayed with what he felt to be true, the mechanical model of the brain.

Carol Dweck (2006) looked at Beck's proposal and went further. Where Beck said that CBT could help people with a wide range of diagnosed mental disorders, Dweck suggested her idea would help everyone with a problem, taking therapy beyond disorder and into ordinary life. Uncontroversially, Dweck said that every person monitors what is happening to them and thinks about its meaning and about what they should do about it, interpreting all these aspects according to a set of beliefs they hold to be true – their mindset. Her research demonstrated that everybody fell into one of two groups: fixed mindset and growth mindset individuals. Dweck claimed that fixed mindset people fail and growth mindset people succeed, so it is important to teach students about their brain and how to change it if they find out they have the wrong mindset. Dweck pointed out that the two mindsets are distinct but there is information leakage between the two, as it is possible to have a fixed mindset and to use growth mindset strategies, which she says actually produce different outcomes to when they are used within the growth mindset. She appears to conceptualize the operation of the brain in same way as Beck (1985) had done earlier (a behaviourist) as a computer with faulty programming, producing the distorted thinking that she and Beck seek to eliminate.

Dweck repeatedly put a great deal of emphasis on the need for sustained hard work and effort to learn what is necessary to make the change from one mindset, represented in the brain as a neural net, to the other. Neural nets are constantly reconfigured as associations between neurones strengthen and weaken throughout the brain. Specialization increases efficiency and greater survival fitness and established nets respond to consistent information to produce similar responses, so habits are formed. Here is the paradox of the plastic brain: it has the potential to be in a state of permanent change and the tendency for any particular pattern of activity to become fixed. If a student has a habit of behaving in a way that does not promote success, any information which the brain identifies as belonging to the physical mind map or neural net will activate it and strengthen the habit and the behaviour. Starting a corrective conversation with a student who has behaved in an unwanted way by rehearsing the problem activates the habit. For an alternative net to become activated the habitual net must be blocked until the alternative net takes over the habitual response.

COMMENT

How could you block a problematic behaviour habit, the failure net?
    Do not pay any attention to it, ignore it, while the alternative success net becomes activated and strengthened.
    How to do that?
    Be solution-focused.

Conclusion

Since taking up solution-support as a teaching approach I have been repeatedly surprised by the rapid change some students have experienced in their behaviour. In this chapter I have introduced some relatively new thinking on the plastic, changeable and dynamic nature of the brain, as a person makes sense of their world and avoids becoming overwhelmed with information flooding in the from inside and outside the body. I have offered an interpretation of how habitual forms of behaviour may be changed to allow other behaviours to take their place. I've brought this interesting idea into the discussion in the hope that it can give you confidence in being, and remaining, solution-focused when you are trying to change complex and apparently intractable problems to do with behaviour. I am not saying the solution-focused approach provides you with a magic wand – in some cases students I have worked with have needed extended support to reach their best hope. That is not to say that solution-support was ineffective, because in all cases students made adaptive changes, but sometimes students asked for more support to keep going with their successful changes.

To use solution-support as a teaching approach you do not need to know the neuroscience discussed in this chapter in depth, or at all, in order to carry out useful work. However, I feel that as professionals we should make whatever connections are possible in order to stand our work on solid footings. In other chapters I have taken a look at some of the assumptions surrounding conventional behaviour management in order to put them into perspective and encourage us all as teachers to break out of the habitual, automatic responses made by some of those who are in positions of high responsibility that may not be in the best interests of students, their families, and teachers.

REFLECTION

Look at this quote:

> Often, for kids with special needs, an element of summary justice is quite useful. If you commit the offence on Monday and don't have the detention till Wednesday, and you have a really good day (in between) – what lesson do you learn? The nearer the consequence is to the crime, the more effective it is from a behaviour management point of view. (Charlie Taylor, quoted in the *Guardian*, 2011)

Appointed as the UK Government's Behaviour Expert for a short period several years ago, Taylor claimed, in asking 'What lesson do you learn?', that

(Continued)

(Continued)

punishment can be 'quite useful' as a way of teaching a student 'with special needs' to avoid repeating the misbehaviour. He described this in terms of committing an offence, of crime and punishment. How would you argue in support of Taylor's claims, and how would you argue against them, given your understanding of current psychological, pedagogical and neuroscientific thinking around behaviour and behaviour change?

References

Beck, A. T. (1985) 'Cognitive approaches to anxiety disorders', in B. F. Shaw, Z. V. Segal, T. M. Vallis and F. E. Cashman (Eds), *Anxiety Disorders: Psychological and Biological Perspectives*. New York: Plenum, pp. 115–35.

Doidge, N. (2007) *The Brain That Changes Itself: Stories of Personal Triumph from the Frontiers of Brain Science*. London: Penguin.

Dweck, C. S. (2006) *Mindset: The New Psychology of Success*. New York: Random House.

The Guardian (2011) 'Schools must engage pupils better, warns Michael Gove's behaviour tsar'. Available at: www.theguardian.com/politics/2011/nov/20/schools-michael-gove-behaviour-adviser (accessed 1 March 2015).

Merzenich, M. (2013) *Soft-Wired: How the New Science of Brain Plasticity Can Change Your Life*. San Francisco, CA: Parnassus.

Neisser, U. (1967) *Cognitive Psychology*. Englewood Cliffs, NJ: Prentice-Hall.

Pascual-Leone, A., Amedi, A., Fregni, F. and Merabet L. B. (2005) 'The plastic human brain cortex', *Annual Review of Neuroscience*, 28: 377–401.

Pink, D. H. (2009) *Drive: The Surprising Truth about What Motivates Us*. London: Riverhead.

10

THE PRACTICAL WORK OF CHANGING BEHAVIOUR

This chapter will give you the opportunity to:

- draw together your new learning and practice
- strengthen your clear, practical understanding of solution-support
- reflect on its application in your own circumstances in the light of additional evidence

Disciplined inquiry for professional development

As teachers, when we go about the work of improving our practice we need straightforward, practical ideas that can be put into action in the classroom today. We also need to know the reason for taking a particular approach in order to feel confident in its use. I hope that by this point in the book you have a clearer understanding of behaviour in educational terms, and how that understanding can help us in planning and carrying out our management and teaching responses.

Throughout the book I have illustrated the use of solution-support in the various case stories, and you will be developing a general understanding of its structure and application.

Now it is time to get specific, about the detailed structure of the approach and about how you can put it into practice in your own context. There is a consistent framework of nine practical steps making up solution-support. The section below will take you along the pathway, but it is important to note that this is not a set script, it is a guide and a map.

COMMENT

Solution-support is an approach to finding solutions, it is not tied down to any particular type of complex problem. Remember that in solution-focused thinking we know that the apparent nature of the problem does not define its solution, as we saw earlier with the student whose problem was described as bad behaviour and whose solution to it was to improve his handwriting. It is an approach that is useful in relation to many different presenting problems. For example, where a student has a problem with learning it is good teaching practice to look for what is already working, and to build on that. My work has mostly been with students whose behaviour has been a concern, but more widely in my team we have used the approach effectively with students who have difficulties with aspects of their learning, rather than their behaviour. For example, a primary school SENCO asked me if the approach could help two students who were falling behind in literacy and who were reluctant to read with a teacher. After one solution-support meeting, involving the SENCO, each student individually and myself as facilitator, both boys started reading with the SENCO and she carried on using elements of solution-support independently to support and track their progress.

REFLECTION

In bringing solution-support into your work, think about using it in a situation which has an element of challenge and where you are likely to be successful. You will know best how to avoid overreaching; use the framework below in the form it is presented at first and build your own success progressively. You could use solution-support yourself, independently for your own development too.

Getting down to the practical work

Good classroom management encourages good learning behaviour. At the outset of your teaching career you can approach it as a management project which requires planning. An approach to project planning, mentioned earlier in this book, is outcome-focused logic modelling, which, while it would require an extra learning effort on your part, could result in a lighter load by helping to structure your management of the classroom.

Solution-support – a framework

In reading through this framework it is important to remember that this is not a rigid script, and you can use the framework in the way that it fits the situation best.

The three beliefs underpinning solution-focused working

Keep these beliefs in mind when you are doing any solution-focused work:

- The student is successful.
- The student is resourceful.
- The student is hopeful.

And a general rule:

- If something's working, do more of it.
- If something's not working, do something different.

Solution-support structure: Checklist

1. Being prepared
2. Setting the scene
3. The project
4. Problem-free talk
5. Goals
6. Exceptions
7. Scaling
8. Compliment
9. Task

Step 1: Being prepared

We are now going to look in detail at how to set up and run a solution-support session, and I am covering all the sections that could contribute to this. Remember, there is no requirement to use all these sections in any one meeting, and a session can work well with just project-setting, problem-free talk and scaling as the main focus. If you have a short time available, do what you can, keeping pace with the student and without rushing; remember less can be more. I have written these notes for one-to-one work with a student, but they apply equally to meetings involving more than two people (e.g. with a student and family members together with school staff). Where I suggest a question that you might ask, this is only to give you an idea of the shape of the question. How you ask it depends on your own way of speaking and matching your language to that of the student you are working with. You will develop your own style with a little practice, and you could use a friendly person to try out your questions on before you work with a student.

When you do your first session it is important to keep notes of the conversation as you go along. I find an exercise book is useful for this and commonplace for students, so what you are doing looks ordinary. Let the student know that you are just keeping notes to help you both remember things, and they can read what you have written whenever they want. This also helps to keep you on track and in the present moment, as it prevents you from writing private comments or analysis. You can use the notebook as a source of information for your own records and leave the original with the student at the end of the work if they would like to keep a record of their success, with a photocopy kept for records if necessary. I find they are usually keen to keep it. The notebook will enable you to track changes together, and to provide feedback. Ask the student if they would like to write in the notebook, draw the scale and so on, to fully share in the responsibility for the work. Sometimes a student has taken on the task of writing the notes themselves. Students are always very interested to look over their story of change and success as they progress towards their best hope. As for the session itself, be clear about how long the meeting will take, keep track of the time as you go, and end on time. If you need a shorter or longer time, negotiate this with the student.

Step 2: Setting the scene

To start off, say a few words about the approach, for example:

> 'We're going to be looking forward, finding out about where you are hoping to get to and about what you are good at.'

As with any teaching, this is about setting out the purpose of the work.

Step 3: The project

Find out what the student is hoping for in school. Ask the 'best hope' question:

> 'What's your best hope for school this week, month or term? What would you notice has changed, when things are going better?'

Ask questions to get a good description of the student's life after the change. If the project goal is about 'my behaviour', find out about what this means to the student. They will know exactly what needs to change for things to go better, so ask about it. This gives the overall project goal. In my experience it is usually something straightforward, like 'my behaviour out of class', 'doing my work in class', 'coming into school on time'.

Step 4: Problem-free talk

Once you have set the scene, let the student know that you are going to put that to one side for now. Ask about something else and inquire into the student's likes, successes, strengths and resources. Find out what the student likes doing, is good at, and about their resources and strengths that bring these successes to life. Reflect back to the student what you have noticed about their strengths and resources. This calls up their growth mind map, the neural net that associates competence, confidence and successes, with the student's perception of school.

Step 5: Goals

Find out what might change to get the student nearer to their best hope, the longer-term goal:

> 'Suppose things are going better, what would you notice that's different? What might change a bit to get you there? What might you do a bit differently?'

This represents the next step, a short-term goal.

Step 6: Exceptions

Find out about a time when the solution has already happened. If the project goal is 'my behaviour in class' you could, for example, ask:

> 'Tell me about a time when you were in a lesson, and you could have started chatting and getting up out of your seat – and you didn't? Tell me about that?'

You may often find the immediate response is 'I don't know'. You can respond to this with some gentle further probing. For example:

> 'That's a good answer; to say you don't know. It's a tricky question. But, suppose you did? Suppose you did know of a time when you could have behaved like that, and you didn't. Tell me about that?'

Finding the exception provides the student with a great asset. It tells them that they are already successful and all they have to do now is 'more of what works'. It makes your job very straightforward, because you now know the solution, and it is already happening.

Step 7: Scaling

Remember that the scale is descriptive, to help the student to track changes and to provide feedback to student and teacher. The student can see their success on paper. It is not a device to force change to happen from the outside, but to maintain the student's sense of autonomy in the work you are doing. When you hear the exception, it is evidence of the solution already happening, it as an early sign of success. The next thing is to find out how it relates to the student's overall 'best hope'.

Use a scale to find out where the student would place themselves right now on a scale where:

1 = nothing achieved in getting nearer to their best hope

10 = best hope achieved

It is likely that the student will mark the scale somewhere above 1, because you have already talked about success in finding the exception, a time when the solution was already happening. Find out what was working at the time, what strengths and resources brought the student's success about. Find out where the student hopes to be on the scale in the near future, tomorrow or next week. Ask the student what they might be doing differently when they are there. If the student should mark the scale at 1, you can still ask where they hope to be in the near future, even 'by the end of our work today'. You might go back to the exception to get a better description of success at that time, and ask the student the scaling question again.

'So how come you are at ...? What is it about you that you can put yourself at ...?'

In the unlikely situation that they consistently mark the scale at 1, you can ask what is called the 'coping question'; a typical way of phrasing this is:

'So even though you say nothing has changed yet, I'm interested to know how come you keep going and don't give up? That you can cope with things as they are?'

Reflect back to the student the strengths and resources that they have spoken about and that you can see coming through their story. A common one that you can highlight is that they have talked to you and engaged in the work you have been doing together.

Step 8: Compliment

Tell the student that you are going to give them a compliment. Check out that they know the meaning of 'compliment' – in my experience many students are unclear about this. Think through the conversation you have just had. What impresses you about the student, what you have heard in their story and the way they have worked with you? You should be able to give the evidence that your compliment is based on, which makes it stronger. Compliment the student and ask them to give themselves a compliment too.

Step 9: Task

Ask the student to notice what is going well for them, let them know that this can apply to things going well in any situation they find themselves in and at any scale. Noticing little things going well is important. Arrange to meet again if it is necessary.

Making a start with solution-support

This is a very brief overview of solution-support. You can list the section headings in the notebook you keep, to aid your memory. There are many descriptions of solution-focused working in schools and elsewhere, and while my framework will correspond with others fairly closely, do feel free to adopt another version of this framework if it suits you better. For a full and accessible description of these sections as they appear more widely in solution-focused brief therapy, see Ratner et al. (2012).

I have given you an overview of the framework so you can see all the possibilities available to you in a teaching session with a student. However, in practice you will develop your skills and confidence over time, as you see how to use the framework and how it fits into your overall teaching. To help you to get started I will give you some specific advice on using this approach, coming out of my own experience in approaching this work as a novice.

Practice seeing all the students you teach as successful, resourceful and hopeful in ordinary situations. When you ask a question and get a surprising and maybe off-beam answer, frame this as the student doing their best to give you the best answer they could give. Ask students to notice what is going well in class and spend a little time collecting their, and your, views of success. You might collect these on a 'What's going well' poster in class. This both reinforces the positive approach you are modelling and provides you with feedback you can use to plan a project around a specific issue in class, where something needs to change. You could use scaling here too, to assess where you are as a class with an issue, and plan the next step.

Is solution-support going to be a useful teaching approach for you? Does it ring true?

The practice-based evidence in this book up to this point comes out of my own experiences over the last 20 years. You might have a question in mind about how the solution-focused approach can be used by a class teacher, and some evidence about that might increase your confidence in its application. In the early 2000s I met a primary teacher, Tim Taylor, who was also researching his work, in his case on the use of imaginative inquiry as a teaching approach. We soon realized that solution-focused inquiry and imaginative inquiry shared common roots, and started to share ideas and practice, something we have continued doing to the present day. With Tim Taylor's permission, the case story below is offered as evidence on the use of solution-support from a class teacher's perspective.

Case story: Ryan

When I first started teaching in 1995 the great behaviour 'guru' was Bill Rogers. His book *You Know the Fair Rule* (Rogers, 1997) was my constant companion and Bill's practical, thoughtful and above all else effective advice was invaluable in helping me survive my first few months in the classroom as a newly qualified teacher.

You Know the Fair Rule is about establishing with the children a set of clearly defined rules, which tell children how to behave in school and allow everyone to live together and get on with their learning. The rules are fair because they are negotiated and everyone agrees to them at the beginning. This is a very effective strategy and I still start the year by creating a contract with my new class. The wording is drafted and agreed and everyone, including the adults, signs his or her name on the contract before it goes on the wall. My job, as the teacher, is to be consistent in enforcing the agreed rules. Occasionally this involves me being a bit mean, which I do not like, but it is my job.

After a while everyone realizes that the rules are fair, they benefit everyone equally and life is easier if they stick to the rules than if they break them. Job done.

Except when it's not.

After four years as a teacher working in an area of severe social deprivation, I had seen three in my class come and go, at different times, all boys and they all drove me close to distraction.

Bill Rogers had helped, but not entirely; he got me and the boys through the year, just, but I was always left feeling it was more through force of will than genuine educational insight. I can't say, hand on heart, those boys learnt much, other than to comply, or that the other children didn't have their experience of education unfairly disrupted. Clearly, I needed a supplementary strategy, not to replace Bill Rogers' ideas – he was still working for most of the time – but something in addition. An entirely different way of working that would help me find a way to reach these troubled children.

It was at this time that I heard about the solution-focused approach from Geoffrey James, who was working for the local authority services as an Advisory Support Teacher. Geoffrey was engaged in his PhD and working with children close to permanent exclusion. He and I talked about how the 'outliers' in my class resisted conventional behaviour strategies and how it was increasingly difficult to keep them in school.

Geoffrey explained that the consistent-rule approach would work fine with the majority of children who understood the benefits of working together as part of a community, but was not useful to a child who saw power as something to oppose. In my experience these children were not prepared to back down, and just kept going until the school was forced to remove them in the best interests of the other children and the staff.

Behaviour management approaches, he explained, depend on the enforcement of authority and only work so long as the person exerting the authority is prepared to enforce it, and the person under the influence of the authority is prepared to submit to it. With a person who refuses to submit, for whatever reason, the results can be a disaster.

Ryan's story

Several years ago a boy called Ryan arrived at the school where I was working. He came from what was rather euphemistically termed an 'Excellence Centre', providing temporary education for students removed from mainstream schools. He was on a managed move as an alternative to permanent exclusion, due to his violent behaviour. I was invited to visit him while he was still at the centre as part of his managed move programme, giving us the opportunity to meet each other before he came to my class the following week.

When I arrived, Ryan was sitting at a table by himself, in a room big enough for nine or ten students. He had two adults with him; one was trying to encourage him to read. Ryan sat with his head in hands, staring listlessly at the page. He didn't look up when I sat down next to him. He looked very young for his six years, especially in a room designed for teenagers.

We spent about an hour together that morning. I tried to talk him about the school I worked in and the things we were learning about. But he wasn't interested. I asked him questions about himself, but I couldn't hear his mumbled answers. I decided to try a different tack and began telling him about the work I was doing with my class at school, using imaginative inquiry.

> *Me:*   We're imagining ourselves as a team of explorers on an island
> covered in jungle. Some people say there are dinosaurs on the
> island, but I've never seen them. To begin with it was difficult
> because we didn't have anywhere to sleep after we landed. But
> we solved that problem by building houses in the trees. It's great
> up there, we can see the whole island if we use the telescope.

Ryan began to show some interest with the faint sign of a smile.

> *Me:*   If you were there, with us on the island, what animals would
> you like to see?
>
> *Ryan:*   A tiger.
>
> *Me:*   I think there are tigers on the island. Probably. What would you
> do if you saw one?
>
> *Ryan:*   Catch it.
>
> *Me:*   Um. I guess you'd need a trap. What kind of trap would you use?
>
> *Ryan:*   One with a cage.
>
> *Me:*   That should work. Why don't we draw it?

For the rest of the time we drew a plan of how to catch the tiger, and I asked
Ryan questions along the way.

> *Me:*   So what do you think we should use to attract it? Who did you
> say would be holding the rope?

When I left, Ryan kept the picture.

I had hopes he would enjoy coming to our school. We had designed a
plan for him, which involved a one-to-one helper, a nurture room he could
go to when he wanted, and regular visits outside school, to go to the park
and run errands for the head teacher. Our aim was to start by making
school somewhere he wanted to be and then gradually, by small steps,
integrate him into the normal fabric of the day.

If I had illusions it was going to be an easy process, they were quickly
shattered on the first day. Ryan arrived with a support worker from the
Excellence Centre, he came into the classroom, took one look at the class,
pushed over a chair and ran out the room. He spent the rest of the day
with his one-to-one support in the nurture room.

The next day he didn't come to my class but started a calm and enjoya-
ble morning getting to know the school and climbing on the apparatus

outside. At playtime we decided we would see how he interacted with the other children and asked him if he would like to go outside. He said he would.

The result was not good. As soon he stepped on the playground his muscles snapped tight, his eyes narrowed and his jaw locked. I kept close to him, but in a flash he was gone, running across the playground, heading towards a young lad from reception. When he reached him, Ryan threw out a straight-armed punch, hitting him in the face and sending him to the floor.

The whole playground seemed to stop still in shock. This was something the rest of the children had never seen at our school. The only movement was Ryan still running and me trying to catch him. He finally stopped when he reached the wall of the school hall and collapsed in a heap, his head buried deep in his hands.

What could I do? I had no idea. What words could I use to make sense of what he had done? What was going to happen to him?

With no answers, I sat down beside him. I could hear him crying.

In front of me was the rest of the playground. The young lad had gone, picked up and carried away by teaching assistants who would mop his tears, contact his mum and see him back to class. The rest of the children were getting back to their games, running, chasing and giggling, as they did every day.

Me: You know, Ryan, you don't have to be like that here. We can help you.

And so we tried. Ryan stayed at the school and we started using solution-support with him. Every day we would talk to him about his best hopes, we would help him when things went wrong by always asking him what he thought he could do differently to put it right. And for a time it was hard, both for us and for him. We were set in our patterns, we as a school that put a large premium on natural justice, he with a vision of himself as someone out of control and a victim of his own anger.

But gradually things began to change. Ryan ran away less and talked more. He still got angry, but he became more amenable to reason and less unpredictable. His mum noticed a change and he started making friends, first with the staff and then with some of the other children. He joined the judo club and started playing football. I left the school before he did, and he carried on. He went to on to high school, took exams, and now has a job. I know this because he pops up every now and again on my Facebook page.

COMMENT

This class teacher used solution-support with no formal training, but having seen the approach in action, and having the framework to refer to, he decided to try using this approach with Ryan. I told him he could call me if he got stuck, and that I thought he could use the approach successfully in his own way. In practice he did not call for help.

Previous attempts to change Ryan's behaviour from the outside by control and punishment had not worked, and he had already been permanently excluded from school because of his behaviour. It required sustained effort from his teacher to maintain his solution-focused perspective, and a clear focus on Ryan's potential to succeed, rather than on his failed performance. But the outcome of the work and effort on the student's and teacher's part was that Ryan became, and remained, included and found success in school.

I will end this book with another piece of evidence of change in a complex situation leading to a good outcome. As with Adam, who we met in an earlier chapter, this is about behaviour that limits a student's opportunities by affecting their engagement, not through outgoing disruptive behaviour but in another more hidden way. This is about a student, Gemma, whom I worked with during a long secondment to a child and adolescent mental health service (CAMHS). As is required, the student's case was managed by a consultant psychiatrist, who oversaw the medical support she received, and I contributed solution-support. For me it shows the power of this simple approach to a complex problem, where the student is the agent in her own success, through her own internal motivation to change, in a situation of great difficulty.

Gemma faced several new and major challenges throughout our work together and overcame them all. At the start I asked her to scale her current position with regard to being in school full-time. She put herself at 3. When I asked whether this might change or might stay where it was over the next two weeks, she said 'Stay in the same place'. Consequently, I asked her to look out for herself staying in the same place as her task. It was always her best hope and yet every time we met she told me she had made a change and things had improved. Her clinical psychologist told me that this is what made the difference and made solution-support effective where cognitive behaviour therapy had not proved useful; we were solution-focused, I treated Gemma as the expert in herself, she had autonomy and purpose, and this carried her forward.

Case story: Gemma

Gemma was 14 and had stopped going to school. She had been fine, getting on well and then something had gone seriously wrong. She had found going to school more difficult, had then withdrawn from school and from the outside world. She was referred to the local CAMHS, where I was providing educational support in my job as a seconded advisory support teacher.

We met in a softly-lit room in the CAMHS clinic, Gemma was sat between her mum and dad, and Dawn, a clinical psychologist and myself were present. We greeted each other and Dawn said that she had invited me to this meeting because I was involved in education as one of the mental health team, and she thought that my approach might be useful to Gemma. Dawn had told me previously that she had started Gemma on CBT, but she had not engaged with it and it had not helped Gemma at all. Dawn thought that maybe the solution-focused approach might suit Gemma better, because it might avoid the anxiety she felt at being required to make changes to correct her habitual wrong-thinking.

Me: Gemma, Dawn asked me if I could come to your meeting today because I'm interested in you and your education, and in how you see things going for you. So I am going to ask you a question: what's your best hope for your education?

Gemma's parents looked at me and at her. Education was a difficult subject for Gemma to think about, let alone talk about to a new person. I waited.

Gemma: I hope that I'll be in school full-time in September.'

Her parents looked surprised, looked at me.

Me: Mmm I see ... your best hope for your education is that you'll be in school full-time in September. Is that right?

Gemma: Yes.

It was May, four months to the start of Year 10.

Me: We could do some work together on that, on your best hope to be back in school full-time in September. Would that be useful for you?

Gemma: Yes.

Me: Shall we do that?

Gemma: Yes.

We got started immediately and met once every two weeks until the end of the summer term.

In early September, the start of the new school year, I enter the clinic and walk through the waiting area to the main desk, for my 9 am appointment with Gemma and her mum. They are already there, waiting to meet me. Gemma is wearing her full school uniform. I hardly need to ask: her imagined best hope has come true. She is back in school full-time.

Conclusion

With the kind cooperation of the students I met and worked with, I have had the wonderful experiences of seeing children and young people flourishing in my presence. My thanks are to them. This book has been about what happened between May and September in Gemma's life, reaching her best hope to be back in school. It has been about Adam and his plan, getting happiness back into his life in school, and the other students you have met through these stories. The book is for all those students in schools who, like Gemma and Adam, face challenges to their education and overcome them, against the odds. And it is for you, a teacher, helping students to succeed and be happy in the moments of their lives you will come to share.

References

Ratner, H., George, E. and Iveson, C. (2012) *Solutions-focused Brief Therapy: 100 Key Points and Techniques*. Abingdon: Routledge.

Rogers, B. (1997) *You Know the Fair Rule: Strategies for Making the Hard Job of Discipline in Schools Easier*, 2nd edn. London: Pearson.

INDEX